SARATOGA
150 YEARS

A HISTORY OF SARATOGA, WYOMING
Elva Evans

Please enjoy.
Elva Evans

PUBLISHED BY CINDY LOOSE,
VISIONS IN PROGRESS (V. I. P.) MARKETING, LLC
SARATOGA, WY

All photographs courtsey of Martin/Perue collection.
Front cover design by Cindy Loose.

© 2020 by Elva Evans
All rights reserved.
No part of this publication may be reproduced in any form, or by any means, electronic or mechanical, including photocopying, recording, or any information browsing, storage or retrieval system, without written permission from the publisher. Address all inquiries to: Visions In Progress (V. I. P.) Marketing, LLC P. O. Box 178, Sarataoga, WY 82331

About the Cover

Skip Glomb painted this painting while living in the valley in 1979. It shows the Overland Trail as it circles down from Elk Mountain to North Platte Crossing. The wagon master on the horse is pointing south and telling the young emigrant family about the hot springs and the valley land which would soon be available for settlement.

Glomb grew up near Jackson Hole. He was a former rodeo cowboy, hunting guide and outfitter—but he always carried a sketch pad in his saddle bag. In 1954 he was commissioned to paint a bucking horse on a cow foreman's bedroll, and his career as a painter and a sculptor gradually took off. His first oil was sold to Teddy Roosevelt's daughter, Alice.

He had sold numerous paintings, sculpted 100 bronzes and was scheduled to do a large bronze for the All-Around-Champion of the Professional Rodeo Cowboys National Rodeo Finals when he was killed near Wheatland on May 30, 1988 when he crashed in his vintage stagger wing Beach Craft airplane "Old Yeller."

Acknowledgments

My family, especially my husband Valle and daughter Kelly Christman, have been extraordinarily helpful. Kelly typed the manuscript; Valle, descended from pioneer ranchers, answered so many questions. He was my "rock."

`Dick Perue, accomplished Saratoga Sun publisher, edited and advised. His historical photograph collection added much to the narrative.

Cindy Loose, V.I.P. Marketing, designed the cover and prepared the manuscript and pictures for the publisher. She is a marvel.

The Saratoga Suns (1891-2020) have been my chief source of history. I wrote Reflections From Our Files (25, 50, 75, and 100 years ago) for the Sun for 23 years. Publishers J.F. Crawford, R.I. Martin, R.D. Martin and Dick Perue had great interest in history and the Sun's pages were packed with history and a diary of weekly incidentals. I had always believed that history should be saved up to the present; this belief spurred the writing of Saratoga's long history.

Rawlins newspapers, the Casper Tribune, the Encampment Herold and Wyoming Wildlife, Sports Afield, American Legion and National Geographic magazines were helpful.

Interviews were especially helpful and enjoyable. (I wish I had done much more.) They were from: Mary Aden, Len Bensen, Chuck Bartlett, Paul Breniman, Jim Copeland, Tex Corpening, Gary Erwin, Leona Evans, Joe Glode, Renee Grubb, Grace Healey, Rich Hepner, Vivian Jones, Colleen Kralick, Swan and Margaret Olson, David Paddock, Hack Patterson, Mary Parker, Margaret Pearson, Josh Peck, Garvin Price, Cecil and Victor Ryan, Bill Schroeder, Richard Sharp, Charles and Carl Sjoden, and Florence Yoakum.

Manuscripts and reports: Report for Forest Atlas by John H. Mullison 1909; Jones-Williams Ranch by Jnell Willford; Herman Werner history from Pat Rhodes; Garrett Price collection from UW Research Center; Forest Service Memorandum by Bruce Torgny 1931; State Water Engineer John Whiting's findings 1927.

Books: Annals of a Former World by John McPhee, 1981, 1988; Colorado's Hot Springs by Deborah Frazier George 1948-1996; Geologic History of Medicine Bow Mountains by S. K. Knight 1990; The Grand Encampment by Candy Moulton 1997; Steamboat by Candy Moulton and Flossie Moulton 1992; Legend of Old Baldy by Linda Durbano 2015; Little Piece of Wyoming by Dan Kinnaman 1996; History of Wyoming by I.S. Bartlett; History of Wyoming by T.A. Larson 1978; Medicine Bow Mining Camps by Mel Duncan 1990; Overland Trail by Erb, Brown, Hughes 1989; Pioneer Ranchers by Burns, Gillespie, Richardson 1955; 70 Years of Cow Country by Agnes Wright Spring 1943; The Longhorns by J. Frank Dobie 1941; Fighting the Depression by Thybony, Rosenberg, Rosenberg 1985; Medicine's Great Journey by Smellan and Moffatt 1992; The People's Chronology by James Tragee 1979; Wyoming Water Rights on the North Platte River.

Contents

CHAPTER ONE
Before the White Man Came 1
   Indian country
   Indian Bathtubs

CHAPTER TWO
Trails West 7
   Recipe for Trail Bread
   Overland Trail (1862-1890)
   North Platte Crossing
   Bennett's Ferry (1867-1885)
   The Union Pacific Railroad (1869-present)

CHAPTER THREE
Warm Springs Takes Root (1874-1884) 21
   Hugus-Chatterton Store
   Hot Springs Hotel (1884-1902)
   The Saratoga Bridge

CHAPTER FOUR
Saratoga Grows 29
   Gold Hill
   Grand Encampment (1897-1910)
   Saratoga and Encampment Railroad (1907-2006)
   Saratoga Incorporates (August 10, 1900)
   1900-1910

CHAPTER FIVE
Industries 57
   Ranching
   Lumber
   Tourism

CHAPTER SIX
Changes... 91
   Transportation
   Shively Field
   Saratoga Hot Springs
   Hot Mineral Springs
   Veterans Island
   World War I (1914-1918)
   "The Roaring Twenties"
   "The Thrifty Thirties"
   World War II (1941-1945), Korea, Vietnam
   1965-1990
   Hanna Coal Boom (1973-1985)
   Health
   Education

CHAPTER SEVEN
Later Changes 143
   1980-2000
   2000-2020
   It Takes a Village

Forward

Saratoga's 150 years seems like a long time. There have been many changes since Indians bathed at our hot springs, mountain men trapped our streams and millions of buffalo, elk and antelope grazed the plains.

Our early settlers must have been breathless as they gazed across the high desert land toward the high purple mountains that lined the valley. There would be many challenges in this new land—more than they realized.

The Upper North Platte River Valley is known for its amazing geology and archaeology. The North Platte River flows through it; without the river and its tributaries the valley would have been destitute and our ranching, lumber, and tourist industries would not have been developed.

Miraculous hot springs determined Saratoga's location, and because it was in the middle valley it became a trade center.

"You have a wonderful history. Everything happened here," a visiting friend said. This is true! It has been an honor to write its history; I hope you will enjoy reading this book. Dick Perue's historical photographs greatly enhance the story.

Elva Evans

SARATOGA 150 YEARS

CHAPTER ONE

Before the White Man Came

The upper North Platte Valley in south central Wyoming, the North Platte River and high mountain ranges had for thousands of years been a seasonal retreat and hunting paradise for the Indians.

We often joke that we live in a "banana belt" because we feel it is milder here than out on the flats. It's possible that Indians had winter camps here because there was grazing, water, wood, shelter and plenty of wild game.

INDIAN COUNTRY

Eight to twelve thousand years ago, Paleo Indians, afoot and carrying few possessions, visited the Medicine Bow mountains. Forest Service archaeologists have found a campsite at a location they have not disclosed and have radiocarbon tested its age.

The mountains were a wonderful summer and fall retreat where they could prepare for long winters by gathering roots and berries, hunting game, drying meat and tanning hides.

In the higher foothills there were rare woods that were used for making bows. Anything very good for its intended purpose was called "good medicine;" therefore, the eastern mountain range was named the "Medicine Bows."

Spanish conquistadors explored and dominated the Americas for several centuries and brought horses with them, which often escaped and multiplied. In the early 1700's horses became the prized possessions of the Plains Indians and their lives completely changed. No longer nomads, afoot and with few possessions, they developed a Horse Buffalo culture with wealth measured by the number of horses each possessed.

Free roving tribal members raided fur trappers and prospectors who had not only horses but also much-prized guns, ammunition, knives and iron pots.

Early white men reported that the Indians were remarkably friendly, and there are no records of hostilities, except for the killing of trappers on Indian Creek in the late 1870's and an 1873 attack on a tie drive. There was, however, hostility between tribes for control of the valley's hunting grounds.

INDIAN BATHTUBS

There are much-cherished mineral hot springs at Saratoga. Melted mountain snow seeps downward through cracks in the earth's crust to the deep, deep fiery magma depths where they are heated, then pressurized upward through faults, finally emerging as hot springs.

The Indians came to these springs on the east banks of the North Platte River where they scooped out the sediments deposited by wind and flooding river waters, then soaked, prayed and rehabilitated.

Faithful to common Indian belief, this natural miracle was neutral ground for about five miles in all directions. Animosities were forgotten, and there was peace here for "good medicine."

The tribes made their last trip to the springs in 1873. While camping and begging at Fort Steele, they contracted smallpox from an eastern emigrant. The Indians had no natural immunity to the disease or any knowledge of contagion, and the smallpox spread quickly among them. They brought their afflicted by travois to the sacred healing waters and followed their ritual of a hot bath followed by a plunge into the river's cold water. Still the patients died, and the surviving Indians left, never to return; they believed that an evil spirit had entered the waters, making it "bad medicine."

Old Indian Bath Tub with town of Saratoga in the distance, ca 1910

When Jim Baker, who frequently trapped here in the 1840's and 1850's, and other early white visitors saw this formation they named it "The Indian Bathtubs." This story is firmly backed by stories told by old mountain man Jim Baker, archeologist W. H. Reed, who first came here in 1868 to study and explore, and by 1860's prospector, John Mullison.

Jim Baker, mountain man, ca. 1873

A 1910 photo labeled The Indian Bathtubs seemed a mystery until the author, while researching and writing Reflections From Our Files, found articles in the Saratoga Sun newspaper files that described these mysterious springs, and further research from the State Engineer's office further confirmed those findings.

People had generally believed that Saratoga's hot springs were of insufficient quantity for any large resort development. But six years after the State of Wyoming purchased the 440 acres in

1921, State Engineer John A. Whiting was sent to inspect the property and examine the hot springs.

Whiting found three spring sites with little flow. He recommended naming the area Saratoga State Park and hiring a landscape architect to design a park. A bathhouse would be included.

The state hired S.S. Sharp, a man they knew well from the time he had spent as a civil engineer in the Cheyenne office. He graded and shaped the boulevard style park in early 1929, but there were suspicious drainage problems at a site (Saratoga Resort driving range) near the present lumber mill. Sharp contracted State Geologist Marzel who came to look, and he agreed that the site required excavation.

Sharp began exhumation on the cattail covered and bubbly-warm spring site, and progress was ardently reported by Sun editor R.I. Martin.

> June 5, 1929: "Excavation revealed an estimated 200,000 gallons of hot water per day flowing from the spring."

> June 20, 1929: "When three feet of heavy mud was excavated, a gusher appeared. Water doubled to a half million gallons a day; its temperature was 113 degrees."

> July 11, 1929: "The problem now is a great oversupply of water making concrete work difficult. The spring water has increased to one million gallons a day."

Sharp wanted to build a 10-foot concrete wall to corral about 15 springs in a 15 foot space. A large centrifugal pump driven by a Fordson tractor that pumped water through a four-inch pipe into a nearby ditch was barely able to keep up with the flow. Sharp needed to reach bedrock to get anchorage for the wall.

But what could they do with so much hot water? Some could

be piped to the new bathhouse. Drainage ditches didn't solve the problem, and the water buildup was hampering the planting of yellow pine trees on the State's new park.

The Denver landscape architect visited, and a few days later workmen dynamited the spring. It was completely destroyed at bedrock.

There were other smaller springs on the property that were likely used by the Indians for centuries. One is capped and under the bluff north of Pic-Pike Road. There are some near the State bathhouse site, and a large capped site lies in the river bank near the bathhouse--which affects the flow in other springs, including the present Hot Pool.

CHAPTER TWO

Trails West

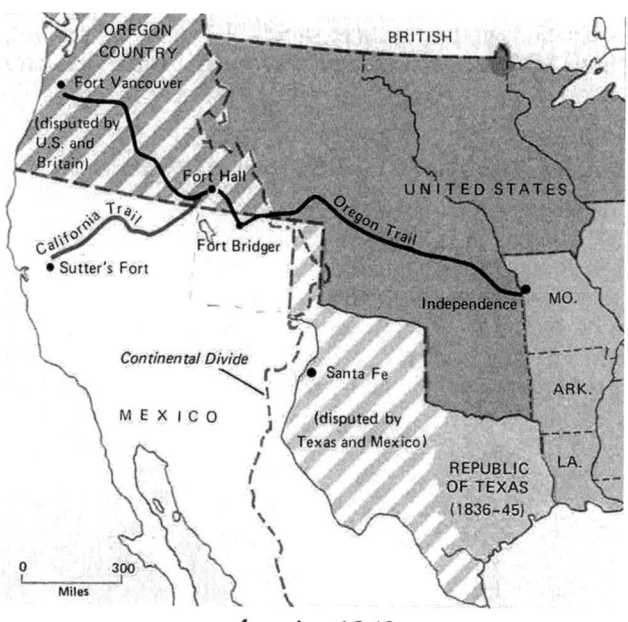

America 1849

T his was a young, ambitious nation in 1783 when George Washington spoke of a grand vision for America in his farewell address. The French and Indian War had settled the northern boundary with Canada and had made the country secure from the Atlantic Ocean to the Mississippi River.

France's Napoleon was fighting for domination in 1803 and was glad to accept $11 million for the 900,000-square-mile territory in the American interior that became the Louisiana Purchase—land that extended from the Mississippi to the summit of the Rocky Mountains. Spanish Florida became our property in 1818.

President James Monroe preached national expansion "from sea to shining sea" in the Monroe Doctrine, which popularly became known as "Manifest Destiny." The remainder of the present-day continental United States was claimed by Mexico.

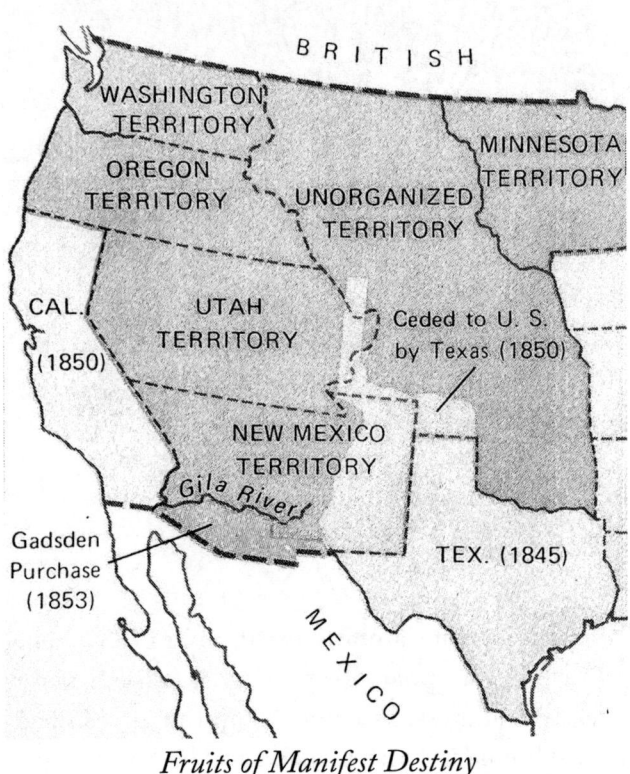

Fruits of Manifest Destiny

A large block of land on the northwest corner of the Pacific was sparsely settled and was up for grabs. It was called Oregon Territory—presently the states of Washington and Oregon. Our leaders encouraged homesteading there, but they secretly eyed coastal California where bucolic Mexican rancheros ran herds of cattle, and small farming and fishing villages dotted the coast. It was far from Mexico's government and received little attention.

Mexico, however, was interested in their Texas land across the Rio Grande River; they declared war when white settlers spread across the area, insistent upon annexing Texas into the Union. After a vicious 16 month war America was victor and in exchange for $15 million dollars became owners of Texas, New Mexico and California territories. The Manifest Destiny became a reality with today's boundaries in place when America treated later with Britain for Oregon Territory.

> **THE COWARDS NEVER STARTED**
> **THE WEAK DIED ON THE WAY**
> **ONLY THE STRONG ARRIVED**
> **THEY WERE THE PIONEERS**

OREGON TRAIL

In 1841 a trickle of traffic began on the trip to Oregon. The overland trip from Independence, Missouri to the Pacific was a difficult six-month journey that began in early spring. Most emigrants were strong, healthy and enduring individuals. About 30 percent were farm families, young to middle-aged, sometimes traveling with kin or friends. Others were tradesmen, professionals, prospectors or adventurers.

The western land had been explored, and mountain men had

trapped its waters. Fort Laramie and Fort Hall were established trading posts and the government had treatied with the Indian tribes for permission to cross their hunting grounds. A wagon trail had not yet been developed, however, and there were rivers, deserts and mountains to cross.

Stories of emigrant suffering were told and retold. A common expression often heard during the trail years was "We have seen the elephant and heard the owl." This meant they had experienced everything that could be imagined.

Guidebooks to the journey recommended a strong wagon capable of carrying 2,500 pounds over rough terrain. Provisions for a family of four included 600 pounds of flour, 400 pounds of bacon, coffee, sugar, lard, beans, dried fruit and whiskey. The addition of tools, guns, ammunition, cooking utensils, bedding, tents, candles, soap, clothing and other essentials left little room for passengers, so most walked.

Eight oxen (male, castrated cattle), or six mules were recommended draft animals. Oxen were preferred because they grazed well. Some emigrants brought a milk cow, extra pulling stock, saddle horses and other livestock. Occasionally an extra hand came along to help drive an extra wagon or herd animals. The men assumed huge responsibilities, caring for animals and wagons and sharing night watch, but they gathered strength from the camaraderie of their fellow travelers. They couldn't succeed otherwise.

For the women, many of whom had reluctantly left home, friends and family, the trip was difficult. Determined to remain positive rather than lose their minds, they hemmed up their skirts, put on pantaloons or donned their husband's trousers, and trudged along the dusty trail through storms, wind and stark, high-altitude sunlight.

The emigrants traveled 12 to 15 miles per day. They started

out at 7 a.m., rested and grazed their stock at noon, then traveled until evening. They occasionally took a day or two off to make repairs or chase loose stock. This gave the women time to wash clothes and cook.

RECIPE FOR TRAIL BREAD

Stir together liberal quantities of soda and warm water. Add flour and salt to make a firm dough. Knead in a large tin pan. Flatten to one inch and place in a Dutch oven with a lid and bake. You can let dough rise at night and fry it in small cakes in the morning.

> "By the time one has squatted around the fire and cooked bread and bacon, washed the dishes and gotten things ready for the next day, some of the others already had their night caps on." - *Casper Star-Tribune, 1993, Women's Voices from the Oregon Trail.*

(Sourdough could also be made from fermented soda and flour (Fleishman's yeast was not brought into the United States from Germany until 1868.) Beans were soaked, then baked all night in a Dutch oven buried in the coals of the campfire.

Nearly a half-million people lived west of the Continental Divide by 1860. Organized freight lines brought supplies, and stagecoach companies carried passengers, mail and express to the West over the Oregon Trail. Traffic greatly increased after 1847 when Mormons began crossing the plains and settled the Great Salt Lake Valley. The Latter-Day Saints church was founded in 1830 by Joseph Smith, and the membership grew, but it was a controversial religion and was not welcome in New York or Illinois where it first took root. When Smith was killed in 1844 by a mob in Illinois, the new leader Brigham Young, determined that they must find unsettled land in the West. The first wave of

Mormon migration began in 1847 and veered southwest from the Oregon Trail. When Young and his followers reached a precipice above the Great Salt Lake Valley, they knew they had found their "Deseret." More wagons followed, and some of the migrants made the journey using handcarts. Salt Lake City subsequently became an important link in the western migration.

Gold was discovered at John Sutter's mill on the American River in the foothills of the Sierra Nevada Mountains in 1848, and it started a gold rush such as was never seen before. Twenty thousand gold seekers, all in a hurry, started out in the spring of 1849, hoping to strike it rich panning for free gold in the streams of the Sierras. Some found the hoped for wealth, but most did not and went home or continued prospecting in other parts of the western mountains.

The 1841 treaty with the Plains Indians only allowed the right of passage through their hunting grounds. The trickle of traffic in 1841, however, became a flood of traffic during the Mormon migration to Utah and the subsequent gold rush to California. The thousands of covered wagons and livestock on the trail cut a huge, ugly ten-mile wide swath through the Indian lands, primarily caused by livestock grazing, often as far as five miles off the trail.

The immense herds of buffalo, estimated in the millions of animals, sensed the tumult and disruption and avoided the trail by going either north or south of it.

Greedy buffalo hunters, who knew about the lucrative markets for buffalo robes and shoe leather, came on the scene in the 1850's. The hunters slaughtered the buffalo, taking only their hides and leaving the carcasses to rot. The Indians were left desperate and destitute by the carnage because the buffalo furnished nearly their entire livelihood. By 1883 only a few hidden pockets of buffalo remained, and bone hunters picked up the last dry bones in Kansas and sold them for fertilizer and use in bone china.

The buffalo has now been designated as the United States' National Mammal. About 5,000 are currently protected in Yellowstone National Park, and there are smaller herds on ranches and Indian reservations around the country.

OVERLAND TRAIL (1862-1890)

The Indians were determined to stop the trespassing and carnage on their hunting grounds. The allied Arapahoe and Cheyenne from the southeast and the fierce Sioux from the north furiously attacked the Oregon Trail and threatened its closure.

The Postmaster General and Ben Holladay's Overland Mail and Express Company searched for and found an alternative route to the south. The new Overland Trail veered from the Oregon Trail at Julesburg, Colorado and followed the South Platte River, winding upward through the Laramie area and west through Bridger Pass.

Fort Halleck was built at the north base of Elk Mountain in 1862. The 1,400 soldiers stationed there were assigned to protect travel on the new trail.

By July 1862 Ben Holladay had moved his stock and paraphernalia to the Overland Trail. "Home" stations were built every 50 miles and provided food and bed space for stage passengers in addition to fresh horses. "Way" stations, 20 miles apart, provided fresh horses.

Some travel persisted on the Oregon Trail because it was a shorter route. Nevertheless, Fort Halleck counted 4,000 wagons and 50,000 head of livestock on the Overland Trail one season. Fierce Indian attacks followed.

Overland Trail near North Platte Crossing, ca. 1874

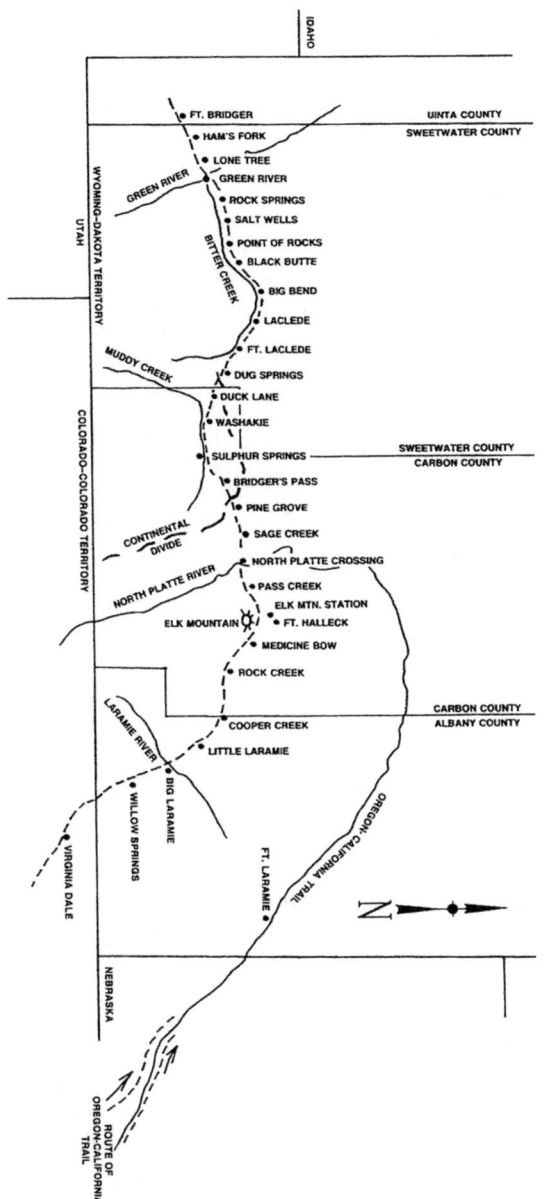

Overland Stage Route,
Erb, Brown, Hughes 1989

NORTH PLATTE CROSSING

North Platte Crossing, ca. 1864 - M. D. Houghton original drawing. Left to right: Sage Creek, wagon crossing over Johnston Island, ferry crossing at upper road.

North Platte crossing is about 12 miles north, downriver from Saratoga. It is a National Historic Place, very interesting but difficult to visit. West of the historic marker on Wyoming Highway 130/230, the road passes through locked gates that require keys and landowner permission to access.

North Platte station was located on the largest river in Wyoming, the North Platte River. It was a home station which offered extra amenities—a telegraph, blacksmith shop, a wheelwright and a store. It was situated in a beautiful area, well protected by high bluffs on the east and south and by the river on the west. Large cottonwoods and a grassy meadow lined the east river bank. The bank south of the river was Ute hunting ground.

A natural staircase from the bottom land gave lookout sentries an entry and a high view of the landscape and potential danger. Travelers carved and wrote their names in wagon grease on the lower cliffs. An old, fenced graveyard sits atop a ridge near the staircase. Graveyards like this one and the many unmarked graves along the trail are testaments to the hardships the emigrants endured.

Johnston Island was located a short way upstream; it was a good wagon crossing when the river was not in flood stage, but livestock were crossed during high water.

Ed Bennett and his partners operated a ferry that carried wagons, passengers and pulling stock. It was a frightening and dangerous experience but woe to the Immigrant who decided to cross on his own rather than pay the ferry fee of $5. Ropes and cables often broke, sending wagons, animals and passengers into the flood waters. No one could save them. Sometimes traffic was held up for days when the water was very high or if the ferry had broken lines and had been carried downstream.

W.O. Owens was 8 years old when his family crossed; he described the scene in later years:

> "Not less than 100 wagons were ferried across that day, and it was an event I shall never forget. I had never seen a ferry before and this one engaged my attention. It was of a pattern typical of those days—the old flat bottom boat held to the cable by two shorter ones and dependent on its propulsion by the current of the stream. By shortening or lengthening the cables the boat could be set obliquely with the direction of the current and the resultant force would carry it over.
>
> "I remember vividly when our wagon, my mother, my two sisters and I were loaded on the boat. And all the way over my mind dwelt constantly on those cables breaking and leaving us to the mercy of the stream."

The ferry went out for the last time in 1867. Ed Bennett and his partners decided the river was too narrow and swift there and moved it upstream—about one mile below the present Pick Bridge. Emigrants had to detour south during high water.

The 1860's have often been called "The Bloody Years on the Plains." C.G. Coutant said that "during the months of June and July of 1862, it was estimated that 75 men, women and children were killed by Indians between Big Laramie and Bridger Pass stations and more than 1,000 head of stock were run off."

One hair-raising incident occurred at North Platte Crossing in June, 1865. The station had been cut off to the west for three weeks by Indians, and mail had accumulated. The superintendent decided to make a night run to get the mail through. Three big coaches were piled full of mail sacks, and they started out at 11 o'clock.

J.J. Hurt, who was a young soldier detailed to accompany the expedition, told about it in later years: At 3 o'clock they passed Pine Grove station where the men in charge had been killed, the station burned and the stock stolen. Shadowy forms moving parallel shot at them. The sun was just rising when they formed a corral with their horses inside and piled up the mail sacks for barricades. They fought all day, and at sundown the Indians pulled off. They had lost horses and men but they hitched up and drove on by night. Once again they were followed by shadowy forms, and within miles of Sulphur Springs, opened up a bombardment. Men at the station came out to help, and they drove safely to the station as fast as their horses could run. They were not molested again.

BENNETT'S FERRY (1867-1885)

Fort Halleck was abandoned in 1866 and moved to the new Fort Sanders near Laramie, the troops being needed as guards for the Bozeman Trail, which Red Cloud's Sioux were bent on closing.

Bennett's Ferry buildings were located 100 yards north of the ferry crossing. It was very important to early inhabitants for travel but also for social and political purposes. Jury trials and elections were often held there.

Military Post at Bennett's Ferry, ca. 1867
Courtesy of Bessie McFarlane Pudge

Howard Corpening, who owned the ranch in later years, has described it: There were log Army barracks, an ammunition building, a blacksmith shop, barn and corrals. It was located northeast of today's Pick Bridge, and a sign "TA Corpening Ranch" marks the site. The road from North Platte Crossing can be seen winding down the hill to the north.

The government began plans for a transcontinental railroad after the Civil War ended. The Indian problem had to be resolved for the massive project; they were given reservation lands and were promised annuities and self-government, but they were natural wanderers and not completely controlled for another ten years.

Bennett's Ferry was used until the railroad was finished in 1869, but the crossing was useful to those traveling by land. The military post was abandoned after the army's Fort Fred Steele was built on the railroad's crossing.

THE UNION PACIFIC RAILROAD (1869-PRESENT)

The far west was rapidly being settled, and there was a great need for supplies and manufactured products. It took freight wagons one year to make the journey; a sailing trip around Cape Horn took six months, and the difficulties and expense of bringing mail and passengers west were tremendous. A railroad would solve those problems.

Two construction giants began building the Union Pacific Railroad in 1867. One started west from Omaha, and the Central Pacific started east from Sacramento, California. They met at Promontory Point, Utah in 1869.

Building was a herculean effort, full of logistics. Surveying, building grade and laying track took 1,000 workers, 5,000 animals and soldiers on guard to protect from Indian attacks with railroad engines bringing ties and rails, sleeping and food cars. It is a wonderful story.

The Union Pacific brought settlement and business to Wyoming. Towns sprang up along the railroad tracks from Cheyenne to Green River. Coal to fuel railroad engines was found at Carbon. Fort Steele was built and Rawlins became our county seat. The Upper North Platte Valley became a place of opportunity for ranching, logging and tourism.

CHAPTER THREE

Warm Springs Takes Root (1874-1884)

William F. Cadwell was the founder of Warm Springs (later named Saratoga). In 1874 he settled the property currently owned by the Saratoga Hot Springs Resort and Spa.

A three-year veteran of the Civil War, he came to this area with his prospecting partner Billy Bauer in 1867. The pair was looking for cash-paying jobs and found work as meat hunters for Overland Trail emigrants and the coal mining town of Carbon.

Game was plentiful in the North Platte Valley, so they decided to headquarter here. In 1873 they started a ranch on Lake Creek and were among the first to register a livestock brand—CB.

Cadwell soon eyed the land around the old Indian Bathtubs as a favorable location for his own ranch; the hot springs that flowed from the river kept a watering hole open in the winter, and there was protection from cold winds and ample grazing.

But Cadwell's ranch operations were constantly interrupted by visitors who needed food and bedroll space. Old time western hospitality required hosts to take in visitors. People's lives depended on this hospitality. So Cadwell's warm little cabin was often crowded with overnight guests.

Before long, Cadwell realized that opportunity was knocking on his door. He added several rooms to his cabin, hired a cook and stocked merchandise for paying customers.

Guests saw the hot springs bubbling up and pined for a rare hot bath. So Cadwell built a bathhouse with two bathtubs built from ship-sawed native lumber. He devised a water pumping roundtable that was powered by an old horse. When a customer wanted a bath, Cadwell yelled, "Git up, Nig," and when the tub was filled, he yelled, "Whoa, Nig."

Cadwell's ranch became a profitable business when experimental cow herds proved successful. Hunting parties arrived and logging began. Settlers began "squatting" on river and creek bottoms until government surveys were made in 1878-1879 and they could file for land legitimately.

Cadwell's little settlement was given the name Warm Springs when a post office was established there on October 4, 1878. Cadwell's store was getting busier and busier and soon a saloon adjoined the store.

> "Monte Blevins from North Park (Walden, Colorado) told about poker sessions at the Warm Springs store that continued night and day for two weeks at a stretch, the players taking flirtations with Lady Luck, and first one and then another would have all the money. When players got tired they would lie down in their canvas-covered bedrolls and take a snooze." - *Saratoga Sun*

Cadwell sold his store to saloon keepers Alter and Miller in 1883 when he began building the Hot Springs Hotel. Cadwell retained the hot springs mineral rights, so hot baths were no longer available. Alter and Miller resold the business within months to W.B. Hugus and Fenimore C. Chatterton.

HUGUS-CHATTERTON STORE

At age 43, Wilbur B. Hugus was already a seasoned

Warm Springs post office and store, ca. 1884

businessman. He had helped his father in his mercantile business in Ohio, and after serving in the cavalry as a first lieutenant he came west and had helped his brother, John W. Hugus, who was a post trader at forts Phil Kearny and D. A. Russell.

When J.W. expanded his large Wyoming-Colorado mercantile and banking business, he sold his Fort Steele store to his brother W.B. and a young clerk named Fenimore C. Chatterton.

Chatterton ran the Fort Steele store, and Hugus ran the Warm Springs store. The partnership lasted until Chatterton left to get his law degree and enter politics.

Chatterton rose quickly in Wyoming politics and was thrust into the governorship when DeForest Richards died in April 1903. In November he refused to pardon Tom Horn for killing Willie Nickels, thus losing favor with powerful Republicans who had hired Horn to discourage homesteading.

He nevertheless had a great impact on Wyoming, leading in irrigation, reclamation, forest and grazing projects. The valley remembers him for his interests in Grand Encampment's mining, and the Saratoga and Encampment railroad. He was also part owner of Saratoga's hot springs and greatly influenced its development.

Fenimore C. Chatterton

Wilbur B. Hugus

Hot Springs Hotel, ca. 1888 – Originally located on the Saratoga Hot Springs Resort's property, in the golf course parking lot by Cadwell Slough.

HOT SPRINGS HOTEL (1884-1902)

Visitors arriving at the Hot Spring Hotel stepped into a wide hall with a black walnut staircase. A parlor, office, barber shop, billiard room, dining room and kitchen were on the main floor. Bedrooms upstairs could accommodate 50 guests. An adjoining bathhouse, livery stable and barn completed the facility.

The new hotel was immediately successful. Word spread and newspapers proclaimed the hotel, "The Pearl of the Platte" and "Wyoming's Great New Health Resort." Guests came from far and wide to stop at the luxurious hotel and take rare hot baths. Individuals with gout or rheumatism often stayed for several weeks while they took the hot baths that greatly relieved their suffering.

The Fourth of July was always a special time. Guests camped on the grounds, took hot baths at the hotel bathhouse, and celebrated together at Cadwell's Island (now Veteran's Island) with Japanese lanterns lighting the night.

Cadwell's Hot Springs Hotel had been built in 1884 for the

enormous sum of $24,000.00; half belonged to William Cadwell, and a quarter to Cadwell's businss partner, M.E. Hocker, a druggist from Rawlins, whose adjoining homestead had been added to the hot springs property.

The elderly Hocker retired in 1888 so Cadwell and Calf Creek rancher James Heather, owner of the remaining quarter interest in the hotel, carried on until 1893 when the keys were handed over to Heather. (We don't know anything about the financial arrangement.) Cadwell also owned several ranch properties, and he resumed cattle ranching until he and his wife moved to a fruit farm near Denver in 1898.

Heather sold the hotel property to Fenimore Chatterton and partners Deal and Rumsey in 1899. There was a mining boom, and Saratoga was developing rapidly.

The Chatterton group had totally refurbished the hotel and bathhouse and reopened when tragedy struck. The Hot Springs Hotel and bathhouse burned to the ground in April 1902! Locals formed a bucket brigade to save their beloved hotel, but to no avail. The fire had started in the bathhouse from an overheated stove in one of the bathrooms. A woman in a nearby bath "barely" escaped the inferno.

There was insurance, but the hotel was not rebuilt. A smaller, white bathhouse and guest cottages were built near the riverbank to the south.

THE SARATOGA BRIDGE

The valley was being settled quickly and its industries becoming evident in the fall of 1885 when Carbon County built a strong iron bridge at Saratoga. The county commissioners felt that a safe and efficient crossing was an absolutely necessity for the valley.

A strong iron bridge was built in Saratoga in 1885

It was joyfully welcomed and appreciated by everyone. It was the only bridge in the valley and firmly established Saratoga as the valley's major business and supply center. The bridge has been replaced several times, always at the same place.

A telephone line was strung from Fort Steele to Saratoga that same year. Business boomed as additional merchandise and special services for patrons were added.

Maude Willford, daughter of Calf Creek pioneers Mr. and Mrs. Henry Jones, was an early valley historian, who described Wilbur Hugus as "exactly the type of individual his patrons liked and understood—blunt and gruff, but honest and dependable." To one housewife who sent an order for a slab of bacon, he replied with a note: "I am out of bacon, so I'm sending you some fine onions." Bacon was a staple and with wild meat furnished pioneer meals.

Government surveys had been completed by 1880 so settlers were streaming in and the Hugus-Chatterton store with its post office and nearby saloon was becoming more and more popular.

William Cadwell could not help noticing his old store's increased business. His new hotel was very popular during the summer and fall months, but business was spotty the rest of the year. His pent up feelings exploded one day when he went to the store for his mail and saw several of his hotel guests eating sardines and crackers. He hurried back to the hotel and hung a sign which said, "Get your eat where you get your sleep, or get your sleep where you get your eat." Upon seeing the sign, the guests quickly loaded up and headed for home.

Then Cadwell built a high board fence on the property line only a foot from the Hugus store's front door. The fence was mysteriously sawed down one night.

When the Cadwell-Hugus relationsip turned sour, Hugus began making an alternative plan. The iron bridge built in 1885 further enhanced his plan.

Heavy traffic over and under Bridge Street bridge, ca. 1885.

CHAPTER FOUR

Saratoga Grows

The Warm Springs post office was renamed Saratoga in 1884. Chatterton remembered visiting an upscale and fashionable resort town named Saratoga Springs, New York in his youth, where people came in the summer to "take the waters." Although the waters were cold there, Chatterton felt Saratoga was a fitting name for our up and coming little village.

Wilbur Hugus, with foresight and business acumen, saw opportunity after the iron bridge was built. He was familiar with the land west of the bridge. He had partnered in a ranch with his Civil War comrade, John Mullison, in 1882; the ranch adjoined the present Saratoga to the north. (A tall white barn marks its location.) He had purchased the nearby Thomas Carpenter homestead in 1884 and the nearby Hassett homestead a little later. These homesteads were sold later in parcels and became additions to the Town of Saratoga. A sliver of land on the east bank of the Platte called the Original Townsite, had been developed around 1886.

When bitter feelings arose between Bill Cadwell and Hugus, Hugus made his next move. He would not be crowded out if he moved his store to the west side. Hugus and Chatterton surveyed 40 acres and laid out streets, blocks, and lots for the Hugus and Chatterton Addition. Rancher John Brewer filled, leveled, and graded the scrubby land. Chatterton left the firm at this point and set up a law practice in Rawlins.

The welcoming business section was placed directly west of the bridge and named Bridge Avenue. Today's River Street was the transportation route south to the upper valley and north to Main Avenue which led to western settlement. This plan brilliantly prevented congestion in the business section, and because the Saratoga bridge was the only one in the valley at that time, many thousands of wagons, stagecoaches, travelers and livestock would pass through in the years ahead. The new W.B. Hugus store (Shively Hardware) on the corner of Bridge and River streets would face the bridge.

Hugus proved to be an astute businessman, a leader and an organizer. He first gave his fellow Episcopalians a lot where they quickly built a church which held its first service in August, 1889. They built a rectory next door and hired a pastor, Reverend R.E.G. Huntington. Hugus traded two lots to some friends for a pair of angora chaps and a sack of potatoes.

He next organized The Saratoga Real Estate and Improvement Company which became a major force in town development, selling lots and developing the SRE & I additions.

Hugus organized a gentleman's social club which built the Sierra Madre Clubhouse on the riverbank at the head of Main Street. That building has been restored and is a recreation retreat for several families.

GOLD HILL

The years from 1889 through 1910 were exciting and turbulent times. Two mining booms rapidly spurred Saratoga's growth.

The new W.B. Hugus store was barely up and running in late August of 1889, when a prospector named Benjamin Arendell arrived in Saratoga with four ounces of gold he had found near the headwaters of Brush Creek in the Medicine Bows. The news spread quickly and soon prospectors arrived with their burros, picks and shovels; they were quickly grubstaked for shares by area investors.

The prospectors spent a terrible first winter at the new Gold Hill camp, crowded in hastily built log cabins and tunneling through ten feet of snow to work their claims. Saratoga residents became worried and sent V.C. Ferguson Livery with supplies. He drove his team and sleigh part way, then backpacked the food and supplies into Gold Hill.

The new Saint Barnabas Episcopal Church and Rectory in background. V. C. Ferguson is breaking a horse on his lot across the street on the present post office parking lot, ca. 1891.

There were 35 to 40 cabins, 200 men, several stores and saloons, a hotel, and a small school there by the next winter, but by 1893 the miners and mining companies had lost their leads in the faulty formations. There were futile attempts throughout the years to revive this over-publicized mining district. Gold Hill was inevitably sold for the taxes in the 1930's.

There were hundreds of claims in the Medicine Bows about that time, but none ever came to fruition. Perhaps Swiss naturalist-geologist Louis Aqassiz, who visited the region in 1867, was correct when he prophesized that our mountains are too badly faulted and folded for successful mining.

There was much drama during Gold Hill's few years of existence. C.W. Scott, who had grubstaked a successful prospector, sold his share in the Mohawk to one of the mining companies for $20,000.00, a tidy sum in those days. He celebrated his good fortune by adding a screened porch and a bay window to his new home on the northeast corner of Main and River streets (presently a new restaurant named Firewater).

There were also sad stories. One discouraged prospector, who had vainly searched for gold in the mountainous west for years, shot himself, leaving a wife and two children. Marie Doebler, during the dark cold winter of 1893, killed herself after a failed love affair. She was buried in Saratoga's new Cadwell Cemetery where her headstone remains.

Within six months after Gold Hill opened Saratoga's population grew from 75 to 300 people. The new west-side Hugus-Chatterton addition was fortunately ready for the building boom that followed; more additions were quickly developed. Water and sewer lines and building restrictions were unheard of in those days. People simply dug a water well, built an outhouse, and threw their dishwater in the yard.

All kinds of people arrived, all looking for opportunity in the new, vibrant area. More stage and freight lines brought visitors and supplies, and several livery and feed stables were built. The new Hugus Saratoga Real Estate and Improvement Company

Burdick–Chatterton brick block (1892) with stages, a saloon and S&E Improvement Co – Gold Hill House building (1889)

office on the corner across Bridge Avenue from the Hugus store, quickly became a food and lodging business and was appropriately named The Gold Hill House.

Two new general stores, built by Franklin Hess and Bob Pilson east of the bridge gave the Hugus store competition. Boarding houses, cafes and saloons opened, and Lyde Willis built a bordello on the northeast corner of Bridge and Second streets.

Many fine buildings appeared after contractors D.C. Kinnaman, Thomas Hood and brickmaster Eugene Kreigh arrived. They were boosted by sawmills, shingle mills and brick yards.

Frame buildings that boast their historic integrity can be seen today: the Episcopal Church and rectory, the Hugus store, the Sierra Madre Clubhouse, and the C.W. Scott and J.B. Maghee homes.

First Presbyterian Church of Saratoga, ca. 1894

Brick buildings that survive are the Hotel Wolf, the Chatterton-Burdick brick block, the present Stolns and Wiant, and the Hood, Kreigh and Condict homes. Sun-dried bricks were made from clay found on Pass and Cedar creeks. The Kreigh home bricks were fired in a kiln.

W. B. Hugus – Shively Hardware Company modern day picture shows the Hugus store facing east on River Street. Photo courtesy of Joe Glode.

Hotel Wolf and the Wolf Annex, ca. 1905

The Hugus-Shively Hardware and the Hotel Wolf are on the National Register of Historic places. There are a number of other significant buildings. A group of local women met with representatives from the Wyoming Recreation Commission to see if these buildings could be nominated, but they were told that there are stricter provisions now—structures must be architecturally significant or connected to famous people or events. However, Saratoga could form its own historic district.

GRAND ENCAMPMENT (1897-1910)

The Grand Encampment mining boom sounded off in July 1897. It was fortunate that Saratoga's west side had been developed and a traffic pattern created because the town was suddenly inundated with investors, promoters, workers and camp followers, all seeking food, shelter and livery service. All through traffic in the years ahead would pass over the Saratoga bridge to the mining district.

Some mines in the southern and western mountains had been developed or were in the process—the Rambler, Portland and Kurtz-Chatterton, and the Yankee Jack and Charter Oak in the Bridger Mining District. By the time the mining boom went bust in 1910, there would be 35 mines. Some would be sold for a nice profit when the finders realized that large capital and mining expertise were needed for deep mining development.

The largest and best producing of the group was the Ferris-Haggarty, which had been discovered by Ed Haggarty in the fall of 1897. It produced a high grade of copper, but its location was problematic. It was west of the snowbound Continental Divide near Battle Lake (on Wyoming Highway 70). The transport of copper ore through 15 feet of snow in winters that lasted eight months was a fearsome prospect. But mining was pursued and freighting began.

It was a 40-mile, two-day journey from the Walcott railhead to the nice little crossroads town named Riverside and a mile further to Encampment. Freight teams needed water and feed every 10 miles, and fresh teams were exchanged every 20 miles.

A half-way station, between Walcott and Saratoga, was established at Midway. It was located in two hollows west of the Overland Trail marker on Highway #130-230. Another halfway station between Saratoga and Encampment was on the southwest bank of Cow Creek on Cow Creek Lane.

Midway Station, half-way between Walcott and Saratoga, ca. 1900

The Saratoga Sun reported that 200-250 freight wagons passed through town each day. They stopped at Saratoga for food and drink. Perhaps they also had a shave and a haircut or spent the night. The horses were watered at the river, and a large barn was built near the present Country Store.

The freight journey from Walcott to the Ferris-Haggarty, then back to Walcott, took about a week. The freight lines brought supplies and mining equipment from Walcott and returned with copper ore. Transportation costs were very expensive, difficult and irregular so mine owners decided to build a 16-mile tramway with high towers and cables carrying ore-filled iron buckets from

Scribner Concord stage pulled by the white "crack six" horses leaving Cow Creek for Saratoga, ca. 1907. Courtesy of Keith Wilcox.

G-string Jack and his freight outfit heading south up River Street, ca. 1907. He operated with a jerk line. A jerk on the right signaled the team to turn right.

the mine to a smelter at Encampment. The tramway and smelter were completed in 1903.

But catastrophe loomed on the horizon. The Ferris-Haggarty was sold and resold to large mining companies. It became overcapitalized and overspent. There were three fires at the smelter—the last one devastating. Penn Wyoming Copper Company went into bankruptcy and receivership in 1910. The Grand Encampment mining boom was over.

Saratoga and Encampment Railway Co.
(1907-2006)

The S&E train crossed two river channels on two tressles, from immediately east of the present Hobo Hot Pool to Veterans Island, then to the west lines of the Saratoga Inn property.

The valley had pressed for a railroad since 1893. Ranching and lumber interests desperately needed transportation for their products, and valley growth required much incoming freight. A link to the Union Pacific was needed to transport copper ingots from the Encampment smelter.

Fenimore Chatterton and his associates stepped in and organized a railroad construction company, which was subsidiary to Penn Wyoming Copper Company, and began building single track, narrow gauge rails at Walcott in 1906. In a hurry to reach Encampment, it nearly bypassed Saratoga, but alert citizens found right-of-way through the hot spring property and persuaded the company to include Saratoga.

S&E Railway in the Encampment River Canyon between Saratoga and Encampment, ca. 1908. Photo by Cecil Ryan and courtesy of Saratoga Historical & Cultural Association.

The Saratoga and Encampment railroad reached Saratoga in August 1907 and the event was celebrated with a huge fish fry. It reached Encampment a year later, but it was too late— Penn Wyoming was on its way down and the railroad went into receivership and operated that way until 1928. The railroad company repeatedly applied to the ICC for permission to abandon because the railroad was not profitable, but valley citizens thwarted those efforts, arguing that the valley needed the railroad. Ranchers had cattle, sheep, wool, hay and grains that needed shipment out; machinery, automobiles and many other things needed shipment in; passenger service was needed for personal and business purposes.

The ICC gave permission for the S & E's abandonment in 1928, and the valley had the opportunity to purchase the railroad for salvage value. It raised the $100,000 and gave the railroad to the Union Pacific with their promise to operate into perpetuity.

R. R. Crow & Co. Planer Mill in Saratoga. Highway and railroad along west side of mill, ca. 1960's

The R.R. Crow Lumber Company built a saw mill at Saratoga in 1934; it was a big boost for the railroad. Railroad tracks were taken out between Saratoga and Encampment in 1977, the depot was abandoned in Saratoga, and the S & E only carried a few cars of woodchips when needed. When the lumber mill closed in 2006, the tracks from Saratoga to Walcott were taken out. The railroad that we had loved so much and had served the valley for nearly a century was gone. It had been a great asset.

SARATOGA DEPOT - SARATOGA MUSEUM

Saratoga people were thrilled when the S & E Railroad built a depot in 1915. The people in this picture are obviously celebrants, newly arrived for one of Saratoga's famous fish fries, a county fair or perhaps a 4th of July picnic.

This improved combination depot housed the depot agent's family, and provided a passenger waiting room, the agent's office and a freight section in the center. It's original location was along the railroad track and immediately west of today's lumber mill.

The Union Pacific gave the depot to the Saratoga Historical and Cultural Association in 1978 with the provision that it be moved. The Saratoga Museum celebrated its opening in 1981 with the Fireside Folk Festival. The Lions Club recreated an old time fish fry, serving nearly a thousand hungry people. Photos courtesy of Saratoga Museum.

The Saratoga Museum began as a 1976 heritage project. Interested people met and elected president Elva Evans, vice president Debby Chastain, secretary Dorothy Rowland and other board members Mimi Gilman, Dan Simmons and Don Erickson to form the Saratoga Historical and Cultural Association.

Historical research began and two publications were distributed. Mimi Gilman's committee helped fund projects with many musical and art extravaganzas. After the depot was given, a huge membership drive began and the depot was moved and remodeled. It opened in 1981 with Evans as volunteer museum director, aided by talented volunteers and guidance from The Colorado Wyoming Association of Museums.

SARATOGA INCORPORATES (AUGUST 10, 1900)

Saratoga was a wild town before it was incorporated. The Spotted Dog Saloon, a curiosity still standing at 313 East Bridge, was one of the town's lively hangouts where men could gather, drink and gamble. Women were not welcomed in saloons, not even prostitutes. There was a small brothel behind the Spotted Dog however. One of the women would sometimes knock on the back door and ask the bartender to fill her bucket with beer for her customers.

Southwest block on East Bridge Avenue, ca. 1910

The remains of Paulson's Spotted Dog Saloon lay east of the bridge on East Bridge and Veterans Streets, ca. 1900.

A temperance hall stood near where ladies served goodies and handed out good reading books to read in a soft chair to save them from the hellish ravages of strong drink.

Some shocking incidents occurred in the spring of 1900 that catapulted the town into action.

A gambler named Harry Durant shot his girlfriend Bessie Wood at a local brothel and hid in a growth of willows where he slit his throat. It looked like he had used morphine to nerve himself.

A crook broke into the Clemmons and Price drugstore a week later and stole money and cocaine. Deputy George (Baldy) Sisson arrested the suspect and threw him in jail, where he tried to set it on fire; he nearly escaped through the chimney.

Still in the six-shooter stage, Saratoga was warned against the tin-horn fraternity's carrying of firearms, but it persisted.

"Lock your doors" was the cry. Theft! Chicken coops were invaded! Fathers disliked it when their wives and daughters were leered at as they walked down the streets. Lewd behavior, intoxication, profane language, fighting and fast driving were other issues.

Saratoga was incorporated by a nearly unanimous vote on August 10, 1900. A. Johnson Doggett was elected mayor; councilmen were C. E. Jensen, C. W. Scott, James Blackhall and Lewis Geis. Town council meetings were held and ordinances were quickly passed with a marshal and night policeman hired to enforce them.

The new Ferris Haggarty Hotel on River Street had an unsavory reputation, and its inmates were told to leave town. The old clothes, shoes and tin cans that littered vacant lots and alleys were cleaned up. Soon peace was restored.

Our first newspaper was the Platte Valley Lyre, founded on June 7, 1888 by George Caldwell. Gertrude and Laura Huntington, daughters of Reverend and Mrs. R.E.G. Huntington, later ran the newspaper.

Another newspaper, the Saratoga Sun, started up July 14, 1891. The two newspapers merged in 1902 and the Sun has been published continuously since then.

1900-1910

Saratoga became a much better town after it was incorporated and a railroad was built. Freight wagons no longer drove through town, and it was safe to walk downtown. Children could walk to school unescorted. On Sunday mornings all you heard were church bells calling their congregations to worship.

Nearly everyone lived on the river's floodplain within six blocks of the business district, so people walked everywhere. Groceries were delivered to the doorsteps by wagon, and a local dairy brought milk each morning.

Life was simpler. A yearly income of five hundred dollars was common, rent was about ten dollars, and meals at a café about 10 to 25 cents. Houses were heated with wood and coal, and a can of kerosene fed lamps. Water was pumped from a nearby well, and an outhouse stood in the backyard.

Housewives worked full-time in their homes; they cooked three meals a day, washed clothes on Mondays, ironed on Tuesdays, and were busy the rest of the week baking bread, cleaning and sewing. Big Sunday dinners ended the week.

The people yearned for the beauty and tranquility of shade trees, flowers, grass and vegetable gardens. Many of the cottonwood trees seen along today's streets were planted then. Hollyhocks and yellow rosebushes required little water and were easily grown. A successful fruit was rhubarb. Most people went berry picking each fall on the creek banks or in the mountain foothills and made delicious jams and jellies.

A Town Hall was built in 1907, and a Babcock fire wagon was purchased. After the highest river flood in history, a levy was built on the west bank above the bridge in 1909.

Taylor Pennock laid out a cemetery on the northeast corner of his homestead in 1895—it was closer to town than the old Cadwell cemetery. The town purchased it around 1900 and has

M. D. Houghton drawing of Saratoga, Wyoming, ca. 1902
Population 1,000. Hot Sulpher Springs, New school with 188 pupils and
3 teachers. Electric plant with 700 lamps. Two churches.

SARATOGA GROWS

Looking east along Bridge Street from Second Street intersection, ca. 1902

1907 Saratoga panoramic

added acreage since then. A cemetery district was formed in 1984 and a 3-mill levy was secured from county taxes. A pavilion was built in 1990, expanded in 2002 and named the Valley Chapel where many memorial services are held. It is a much cherished place.

The valley people had always loved horse races, often with blooded stock. They raced on Main Avenue or on the west hills. There was strong betting and large purses for the winners.

Fourth of July, ca. 1900

The 1900 Fourth of July was especially eventful, with horse and foot races, wheelbarrow, sack, three-legged and bicycle races. A tug-of-war, baseball game or a rock-drilling contest were sometimes held on other Fourths.

A Carbon County Fair Association was organized in 1908 by Hanna, Rawlins and Valley men, mostly interested in horse races. They purchased forty acres of the Taylor Pennock homestead land east of town. (It is presently owned by Rod Bennett.) They grated a half-mile elliptical race track, barely visible now, spruced up the Pennock buildings and put on Carbon County's first fair. Two thousand people attended, many of them arriving by the new S&E Railroad.

Ranchers proudly displayed their fine cattle and horses, and the women vied for prizes on their fancywork and preserves. A 24x120-foot grandstand was built in 1911.

Riding a high one to amuse the crowd.

Wyoming is called The Cowboy State and its symbol is the bucking horse. We proudly display the cowboy and bucking horse logo on our license plates and root for the Wyoming Cowboy football team.

The legendary bucking horse, Steamboat, is shown on the logo with an unknown rider. He was named Steamboat because he had injured his nose and whistled like a steamboat when he breathed hard. The book Steamboat, written by Candy Moulten and her mother-in-law Flossie Moulten, documents the horse and those who tried to ride him. It is a great read.

Steamboat was a jet black, powerfully built and a superb athlete. He twisted and turned in all directions and when he landed it was like a sledgehammer. Only a few road him successfully. This was back in the days when there was no eight-second ride and cowboys had to ride their horse to a standstill. Many cowboys were disabled as a result.

Saddling a wild bronco. The whole world loves the cowboy.

Garrett Price once accompanied his father, Dr. Sam Price (who was our doctor from 1895 to 1912), to an Encampment rodeo. In the afternoon, the doctor was called to one of the rider's (Hugh Clark) hotel room, where Clark was thrashing and yelling in pain. Two men held him down so the doctor could give him medication. The doctor told his son, "I can't do much for him. He's all broken up inside."

Thad Sowder won the first world championship for saddle bronc riding in 1901 at Denver. He also won in 1902 when he and Tom Minor competed in the finals, each riding Steamboat. Sowder often visited the valley and lived here for a time. His brothers, W. H. and O. G. Sowder, were owners of the present Silver Spur Rainbow Ranch.

Sowder, Fred Dodge, Jessie Barkhurst and Joe Peryam were the valley's first rodeo heroes. They performed in Buffalo Bill's Wild West Horse Show and traveled the world. Pulp magazines glorified the exploits of the American cowboy everywhere. Fred

Grandstand at first Carbon County Fair in Saratoga in 1911.

ca. 1950's

Dodge also rode Steamboat; he organized the bucking horse contests for the American Legion 4th of July rodeo from 1922 until 1937.

...

The first decade of the 20th century, while the Encampment mines were still operating, was marked with major town improvements.

The Parr (Waterloo) and the Palace Hotels were built. A large addition, added to the Wolf and the Wolf Annex (Lollipops) with 14 rooms upstairs, was built next door in 1902.

Wilbur Hugus handed over his store keys to his brother John W. in 1892 and moved his family to his Pass Creek ranch. His store, with a two-story addition, became a hardware store, Saratoga Mercantile and a J.W. Hugus bank. It was not long until sheepmen, the Cosgriff Brothers, purchased the building and incorporated the Saratoga State Bank (1899-1987) and placed it in the west end where it conducted business until 1926 when it combined with the Stock Growers Bank and moved to the Burdick-Chatterton building.

Gus Jensen and his brother Carl bought the Burdick-Chatterton brick block for a hardware store and a mortuary. Gus Jensen moved his music hall on Main Street to Bridge Street where an addition was built, and it became the Jensen Opera House where traveling entertainments, dances, social gatherings, meetings, basketball games and boxing matches were held. It was Saratoga's first community center.

A. Johnson Doggett built his store on the corner of Bridge Avenue and First Street in 1900 which later became Pilon's Grocery—Blackhawk Gallery—Laura M's.

A two-story brick school with four large classrooms and wide halls was built on the west bench in 1900, but it was already too small for its 188 students when it opened.

Warren C. Edwards built his saddle, harness and shoe repair business across Bridge Avenue. It later became Whitney's—Hat Creek—and presently Sweet Marie's. Hunter and Laughlin built a furniture and second hand store west of Edwards.

Electricity was brought into Saratoga in 1902 and residents were ecstatic, even though only a single light bulb hung from the ceilings of their homes. Service was provided from dusk until midnight.

Telephones and a switchboard came into town in 1902. The number of subscribers gradually increased from the original 13 until nearly everyone had them hanging on their walls. Young Cecil Ryan hung telephone wire on fence posts to Brush Creek in 1907 and other country lines followed.

CHAPTER FIVE

Industries

Three major industries have sustained the valley for these many years—Ranching, Lumber and Tourism.

RANCHING

Some of the men who had come here in the 1860's stayed and started ranches. They wrote letters home describing this new country.

My husband's family story began in 1879 when B.T. Ryan welcomed his sister Rebecca, her husband William E. Meason, and their six children to the valley. He had urged them to come immediately because the land was being surveyed and would soon be ready for homestead application. In the meantime they could take their pick of the land and have squatter's rights.

While Tom Ryan was running the army's sawmill at Fort Steele, he discovered the upper North Platte Valley and believed there was opportunity here. He moved his young family here in 1874 and began cattle ranching. This was Ute hunting ground; they often came here from their Colorado reservation and were friendly to the ten bachelors living here. Ryan said that white renegades had stolen his cattle once, and when the Utes heard this they tracked the cattle and brought them home.

Will and Rebecca Meason were just getting settled on their

ranch at the mouth of Cedar Creek in September 1879 when a rider came and warned them of a possible Ute Indian attack. Settlers were urged to gather at Warm Springs or the Brauer ranch for mutual protection.

They learned later that the 3,600 member Uncompahgre Utes, encamped on their reservation near present Meeker, Colorado, had become enraged when their agent Ezra Meeker demanded that they begin farming. He had also plowed up their racetrack, where they loved to race their ponies. The Utes killed Meeker and his men, abducted his wife and daughter and rampaged the countryside.

Fort Steele soldiers were called, but were ambushed at Milk Creek before they reached the agency. Other troops had been telegraphed and they quelled the Meeker Massacre. The Utes were moved to a reservation in eastern Utah a short time later.

The early ranchers had been lured here by the 1862 Homestead Act which promised 160 acres if they would build a cabin and maintain residence for five years. But this was different high altitude, semi-arid land, and they had come from places where 160 acres could provide a decent living. Could it be done here?

The Desert Land Act of 1877 greatly increased interest. It provided a 640 acre section of land, purchased at 25 cents an acre, with a residence of three years when another dollar an acre was due. But the act also required that irrigation water must be brought to the land. This was a totally new concept, one they would learn.

The settlers looked up from their original homesteads on the creek and river bottoms and realized that the benchlands above them could be cleared of sagebrush and plowed and planted.

All of this required money and most of the homesteaders had very little money. Land, cattle, machinery, draft horses, harnesses, barns, ditches and corrals were needed. They would soon learn

Cattle roundup near Saratoga, ca. 1885

that fencing was also necessary.

Many of our pioneers were in the prime of life, seasoned to hardship by the Civil War, and in their determination to succeed found ways to earn money. Al Huston, Henry Jones and others guided wealthy hunters. Tom Ryan, the Mowry brothers, and S.S. Wood ran sawmills; John Brewer leveled and graded land. Others grubbed sagebrush, worked on construction, or found other ways to make money.

Many homesteaders became disheartened by the many challenges and sold their homesteads for a pittance to neighboring ranchers. Jnell Willford discovered that the abstracts from the Jones and Williams ranch on Calf Creek contained ten homesteads that had been added during those early years when homesteaders left.

Cattle ranching began when the Union Pacific was built in 1868; it enabled cattle shipments to eastern markets. The cattle industry swept westward from Cheyenne and experimental cattle herds were successfully run here in 1875.

This was a vast, free grazing land with stock water available from North Platte River tributaries. Word quickly spread that profits could be as much as forty percent. Soon big cattle companies were organized, financed by British and eastern U.S. investors.

William F. Swan brought in 4,000 head of Oregon cattle to his Pass Creek ranch in 1881; it was named the El Seven with L7 the cattle brand. The ranch quickly expanded to Lake Creek, Cow Creek and Snake River. Some other companies were the Pothook, Pick, Two Bar and Tomahawk, all named for their brands.

Cattle flooded the range. Many were Texas cattle, often wild and rugged Longhorns that had been trailed up the famous Chisholm Trail, and then sold to aspiring cattlemen. They soon learned that the tall, thin cattle with long horns produced little meat and were only good for hide and glue.

The Longhorns sometimes had six-foot horns, and when they were shipped in crowded railroad cars, they bruised and gashed each other which made the meat less marketable. They were gradually replaced; Hereford and Shorthorn cattle became the favored breeds.

Cattle roundups became necessary when thousands of cattle intermingled on the range. "Reps" and cowboys from the big outfits, homesteaders and other helpers participated in the spring and fall roundups, each one lasting six weeks. The cattle were sorted and the calves were branded each spring then sorted for market in the fall.

Cattle rustling became a problem when cowboys and homesteaders, eager for a start, branded cattle with their own brand or used hot arc-shaped irons to change brands. Cattlemen took the law into their own hands and dealt harshly with them, often by hanging. They hired range detectives who searched for troublemakers.

Branding a Maverick, ca. 1890

The Tom Horn case went down in history in 1901 when Horn was hired by ranchmen and sent to eastern Wyoming to discourage homesteaders who were taking up land and favorite watering holes, and spreading sheep across the land. One morning 14-year-old Willie Nickell, wearing his father Kels' hat and coat, was shot down. Horn was arrested and tried. When acting governor, Fenimore Chatterton, refused to pardon him in 1903, Horn was hung and cattlemen sweared revenge—Chatterton was not elected governor the next term. The Nickell family moved to the valley and ranched on Lake Creek. It is assumed they ran sheep.

1926 Gollings drawing depicting the winter of 1886-1887, courtesy of Bill and Carole Ward

The overstocked range was fodder for the disastrous winter of 1886-1887. A dry summer and fall was followed by blizzards and subzero temperatures that began in November and ended in February. The already weakened cattle drifted with the blowing snow in search of shelter and water and piled up in ravines. The

Laramie Boomerang reported a sixty-six percent cattle loss in the valley.

The get rich cattle bonanza was over, and a major lesson was learned: "the system was a gamble with the trump card in the hands of the elements." No longer could cattle be grazed the year around on open range but must be fed hay during the long winter months. The ranchers needed to develop hay lands, which meant bringing water to the land for irrigation purposes.

Our 1875 territorial legislature showed great foresight in recognizing the importance of water. It gave priority in water rights to "first in time, first in use." In 1886 it formulated a law stating that "water is state property and cannot be sold off the land." Wyoming water laws have been copied by other western states and have given valuable protection to ranching interests throughout the years.

Water is the lifeblood of the West and the essential ingredient that developed valley ranching. The North Platte's tributaries carry melted snow pack from the high mountains, flooding in May and June when our hay crop is growing and water is needed the most.

After finding a water source and filing for rights, the ranchers surveyed the gravity flow and built canals and ditches. They usually partnered with neighboring ranchers.

The North Platte River is fully used and controlled from its beginning at Rabbit Ears Pass in North Park, Colorado, through the North Platte Valley. It flows from Casper through Nebraska and then empties into the Missouri River below Omaha.

The 1894 Carey Act made dry land available for irrigation projects but was unsuccessful until the federal government became involved and passed the 1905 Reclamation Act that made federal funding available for storage dams.

Because our North Platte River is the largest river in Wyoming and has never run dry, not even in the Depression years, 9 large dams and 4 power plants have been constructed on it. When there is water surplus during the months of May, June and July the dams are filled and canals carry water to Carey irrigation projects in northeast Wyoming and Nebraska. The Bureau of Reclamation is the watchdog.

This system works well in wet years, but during dry years it wracks havoc. The ranchers who have lower appropriation dates have to watch much needed irrigation water flow by waiting until it is their turn. Much squabbling and expensive and difficult litigation has ensued throughout the years. Today the State is ever watchful for water grabbers. Several ranches have been sold with plans to transfer the water rights somewhere else. These plans have been thwarted because our laws state that water cannot leave the land for which it was appropriated.

L. G. Davis brought 100 head of registered Herefords to his river ranch (presently Kelley Land and Cattle Company) in 1902 and won many prizes at cattle shows. Ed Sears, who was expert in the Hereford breed was selected as a judge for the Denver Stock Show and mentored his two sons-in-law in the purebred Hereford business.

Soon there were ten purebred Hereford breeders in the valley. They won so many prizes at stock shows that our valley became known as the Valley of Champions.

Cross-breeding began about 1957, when Bill Sidley brought in white Charolais cattle to his Cow Creek ranch. Today's ranchers seem to prefer Black Angus or mixed breeds. It is the quantity and quality of the meat that matters most now—color doesn't matter.

Sheep, or "woolies", were brought into this country by Richard Savage in 1883. Cattlemen resented the smelly, blatting animals that "stank up water holes and ate the grass to the roots."

In an effort to stave off the sheep invasion, masked cattle ranchers drove a large band of Savage sheep off the cliff north of Saratoga, and the cliff received its name—Sheep Rock. This incident was kept secret, but early resident John Eager told about it years later, and Garrett Price (a well-known New York cartoonist and son of Dr. Sam Price) saw the large pile of bones at the base of Sheep Rock and wrote about it around 1905. One of the involved ranchers described the incident to Oregon relatives who passed the story on to his granddaughter in later years.

Cattle-sheep conflicts created chaos on Wyoming ranges peaking between 1897 and 1909, but our local Ranchmen's League sat down for dinner at the Hotel Wolf and compromised by setting boundary lines with cattle south of the line and sheep on the north. Creeks were usually designated boundaries; otherwise, rocks were piled on hilltops to mark separation points. People call them sheepherder monuments, little realizing their purpose.

Cattlemen soon learned that sheep were very adapted to this country. Many ran a flock of sheep and a herd of cattle. Woven wire fences kept the sheep from straying so no sheepherding was necessary, and the rancher appreciated the two paychecks each year—one for sheared wool in the spring and one in the fall for meat from lambs.

The sheep industry became very large in Wyoming, numbering six million in 1910. Carbon County was once the largest producer in the nation. Sheep numbers began to decline, and by 1980 there were only about one million left in the State. Increased grazing fees, market prices, imports, predators, poisonous plants, a labor shortage, and man-made fibers all contributed to the demise of the sheep industry.

The depression year of 1934 was the worst in ranching history. A severe drought with very little snowpack in the mountains stretched through the Midwest and mountain states. Valley tributaries ran dry, and there were no summer rains. Ranchers drilled for stock water and began shipping their cattle that spring. The North Platte River ran at a very low 30 cubic feet per second, fed only by Douglas and Big Creeks. There was a deluge of cattle at the markets, and there were no buyers. The dust bowl states that fattened western cattle could not produce feed. The government stepped in and searched for buyers in other states, but there were few. Two meat canning factories were built in Wyoming, but they could not keep up.

The starving cattle were at last saved from starvation by the government. Crews armed with guns swept the State, and after seed cattle were selected the rest were shot and buried. Ranchers were paid less than ordinary market value—perhaps six to twelve dollars each for the slaughtered cattle.

Dairy cattle had been brought in earlier, but the new County Agent promoted that industry in 1926 with emerging modern methods. Gas generators ran milking machines; sanitation and pasteurization of milk became important.

Dairying was a boom to the small ranchers and those starting up. The industry brought in monthly checks for about 40 years. But competitive eastern dairies, with close grain supplies, modern cooling and better shipping eventually closed down valley dairies.

The Winter of 1949 was another tough time for ranchers. The winter started out mildly but tore loose on January 2, 1949, with six major blizzards, unrelenting sixty mile per hour winds and freezing temperatures for over six weeks. It paralyzed the region, halting traffic. An estimated three feet of snow fell and drifted into snowbanks sometimes twenty feet high. Ranchers struggled to feed their livestock with shovels, pitch forks, teams and sleds. Fifty thousand cattle died, some buried upright in snowdrifts; one hundred thousand sheep were lost. The storm was over on February 19, but it took the U.S. Army and sixteen bulldozers over a month to clear roads.

Predators have always been a problem for ranchers. Wolves were numerous in the 1890's and early 1900's and killed many young cattle, sheep and horses. A pack of three gray wolves nearly pulled John Schoonjan from his horse in February 1896 when he was returning to his Pass Creek ranch through deep snowdrifts. Schoonjan was unarmed that day and with difficulty clubbed them off.

William Turnbull and Jessie Barkhurst took their hounds out often to hunt wolves and were quite successful. The Stock Association began offering bounties of $25 each for wolves in 1906, and the government hired exterminators, "wolfers," who eradicated Wyoming wolves.

Coyotes are numerous and prey on any meat they can find. They will kill sheep en mass for the sake of killing. They were controlled by poisoned bait until it was outlawed in the 1960's.

The Taylor Grazing Act (1934) put an end to homesteading and permanently ended all free grazing; but a host of problems remained, and new ones emerge as time goes by.

Multiple-use is the byword now, but increased recreation, lumber, ranch, coal, oil and gas interests often collide with conservation and preservation beliefs.

Ranching has been very much improved by modern machinery. A man with a scythe, hand-held rake and a wagon could once produce only a few wagon loads of loose hay a day. Eight men, 20 horses and machinery, much of it hand-made, could put up the hay in later days. Now, one man with a swather, haybaler and loader can provide winter hay for 250 cows.

A famous predator case occurred in summer 1971 on the former Isadore Bolton ranch (presently the Overland Trail Ranch).

The ranch had a small beginning as a sheep ranch on nearby

Lake Creek around 1890. By the time Herman Werner purchased the ranch in 1967, the ranch had expanded westward to 150,000 acres with additional government and state leased lands. The ranch roughly covered the checkerboard land from Walcott to Rawlins, and ran 10,000 sheep and 2,500 cattle.

Government trappers had used traps, cyanide guns and poison-filled dead animals to control predators until the 1960's when poisons were outlawed. Werner discovered that predators were killing his animals at an alarming rate that ate up his ranch profits.

Federal inspectors came to the ranch when they heard about helicopter shootings of raptors; they discovered a cache of 360 dead golden eagles and several bald eagles on the ranch. The press reported this to the public, and there was a huge outcry from conservationists across the nation.

Herman Werner denied accusations that he had hired a helicopter service and shotgun marksmen to kill the goldens. The case was brought to federal court, but Werner was released from charges.

Perhaps the public did not realize the difference between the bald eagle (our national bird) and the golden eagle. The bald eagle diet consists of 80 percent fish and 20 percent carrion, according to the *Wyoming Wildlife* magazine. The golden eagle eats fresh meat.

The author and her husband Valle witnessed an unforgettable golden eagle killing one day as they were driving from Saratoga to Walcott.

They noticed an agitated herd of antelope at the highway fence, and as they looked toward a hill they saw a stiff-legged antelope standing as if paralyzed. Mounted near its head was a golden eagle, poised with its talons piercing the animal's spinal cord. Three goldens were perched on light poles waiting for their dinner. An old hunter guide and friend said that he had seen these golden eagle killings a number of times.

Herman Werner

An unsolved mystery of another kind took place in 1975 when Ken Olson discovered a mutilated heifer on his ranch northwest of Saratoga. Deputy Sheriff Glen Glidden came and found a 14 by 2-inch hole in the animal's rear with rectum, sex organs and part of its milk bag removed by a sharp instrument. There was a lack of blood and no sign of tracks. Colorado reported 65 mutilations. Animals were found with eyes, mouth, ears, nose, hides and genitals missing. The public suspected extraterrestrial activity.

A strangely-deteriorated beef animal was found by the Bomars on Lake Creek, and sightings of lighted, saucer-shaped objects flying in the night skies were seen by some local residents.

The Philip Anschutz Corporation out of Denver purchased the Bolton ranch in February 1996. Within a decade they announced that they would build one thousand wind turbines on the ranch; it was later determined the wind farm would be located on Chokecherry Knob, five miles south of Rawlins.

When coal, a huge energy resource, declined, talk about renewable resources—wind and solar—began. Two wind turbines were installed at Medicine Bow in 1982, and other projects at Simpson Ridge, Arlington and Elk Mountain followed. Wyoming has been ranked among the four best states for wind production because its wind is more constant.

The Chokecherry and Sierra Madre wind farm is projected to be the largest in the United States; it has been through a twelve-year permitting process and many public hearings that revealed a nation-wide concern for wildlife, particularly potential eagle deaths caused by rotating propeller blades. The project is moving forward, and wind power is gaining in popularity. Turbines are being improved so that wind energy can compete with other energy sources.

LUMBER

Our lumber industry began in 1867 when the Union Pacific was building its railroad through Wyoming. The U.P. needed millions of wood ties on which to lay its tracks, and in our forests there were long, straight lodgepole pine trees.

J.C. Teller began logging operations on the western slope of the Medicine Bows in 1867. Other companies followed, and they all selected their cuts wherever they pleased.

Turning ties loose from landing on French Creek, ca. 1920's

Experienced "tie hacks" were usually each assigned 100-foot logging strips, where they cut down trees, sawed them into 8-foot lengths, then hacked and hewed them with broadaxes into 4-sided ties. Men who were "skidders" hauled the ties to creek-side "landings" where they were piled until spring when the "tie drive" began.

These woodsmen had learned the age-old method of water transportation. They selected their cut on the more navigable Douglas, French, and Brush creeks. When spring thaws and the proper stream flow appeared they began the Herculean, dangerous and methodical tie drive down the creeks to the North Platte River, thence to Fort Steele where a strong "boom" built of ties and cables held the ties until they were taken from the water at the tie-loading plant and sent by rail to U.P. building operations. (In later years the ties were sent to Laramie for treatment that made them last longer.)

Whitewater men poke and prod ties downstream with pic-pike poles.

The six to eight-week tie drive began in May. About 100 men assembled on the upper creek landings and were assigned into groups: A "lead gang" that removed obstacles and prepared a series of dams; "whitewater men", experienced and agile, who prodded and directed the ties downstream and broke up tie jams; "rear monkies" who guided stragglers; and "slough hogs" who pulled and carried stranded ties back to the stream. They all wore wool clothing that was warm even when they were wet; their boots were embedded with cleats for safe footing.

The dams were constructed with 4-sided log cribs filled with rock, and upright logs were placed between cribs. A log spillway in the middle could be opened, and water buildup transported the ties to the next dam.

Cook and bedding wagons were driven down the stream to the next campsite. When the ties reached the river they were held in a "boom" until the river reached the correct height. If it was too high the ties were carried over the riverbanks to hay meadows and ranchers became agitated.

A boom held the ties while the tie drivers celebrated Togie Day, ca. 1935

As the tie drive approached Saratoga, there was a loud cry "It's Togie Day"; seasoned drivers rode jubilantly with each foot on a

Rear Monkies clean up the tie drive's mess as they approach Saratoga, ca. 1935

tie to the Saratoga Bridge where the townspeople had gathered to witness the spectacle.

Saratoga was ready for a five or six day party with extra barrels of whiskey and newly-arrived fancy ladies. The disembarked tie drivers hurried to the nearest saloon. People talked for years about the grimy men with sloppy hats and studded boots who laughed, danced, sang and told stories while they downed their whiskey, unaware that they were shredding the wooden floor with their boots. Tie drivers from other camps arrived later, and Saratoga experienced a booming spring business.

Tie drives ended in 1940, when the Union Pacific announced they would no longer accept sand-encrusted irregular ties.

B.T. Ryan's sawmill in Ryan Park was the first sawmill in the area, ca. 1890

Ralph R. Crow came to the valley in 1928 and was quick to sense a change in the lumber industry. He soon had nine portable sawmills, each operated by seven men, that could be moved to different logging sites. They produced perfect four-sided ties that were seven inches thick, nine inches wide and eight feet in length. The loggers lived in "skid cabins" while they each cut logs on their timber strips. Their cabins were built from "slabs" (the cut sides of logs) and could be skidded by horse teams to new locations. Trucking gradually replaced tie drives, and Crow built a sawmill in 1934 by the S and E railroad track in Saratoga, where the Erwin sawmill is located now.

When Crow purchased the large Barrett Ridge timber sale in 1930, he selected a site for headquarters and a permanent logging camp—Ryan Park. It was named for B.T. Ryan, who had operated his sawmill there. It became a happy, thriving little community by 1935 with a school, post office, store and a cookhouse where single men were fed.

R.R. Crow & Co. Sawmill at Crow Creek Landing, ca. 1960

A "watering hole" named Ten Mile was built down the road; it was the scene of many accordian-playing and rompin' stompin' dances where loggers and valley people gathered.

But more changes came by the 1950's when an oiled highway and improved trucking lured families into Saratoga and Encampment. Ryan Park became a weekend retreat and then a community of summer and permanent residents.

Medicine Bow Lodge opened in 1918, and has continuously operated since then. Jessie Moore (Mrs. Charlie Plummer) Saratoga's first telephone operator, had long-dreamed of a rustic mountain resort on this side of the "Snowies" where guests, accompanied by guides, could hunt or fish in the mountain lakes on horseback. The lodge was built on Barrett Creek, a few miles below Ryan Park. Snowmobilers from Laramie often use it as a destination now.

Barret Ridge Ski Jumping at Ten Mile, ca. 1940's

The Brush Creek Ranger Station, built by the Civilian Conservation Corps in 1939, is a National Historic Site. It is located on Highway 130 opposite the lodge turnoff.

The Medicine Bow National Forest was established on May 22, 1902, resulting from persistent outcries from valley residents who said our forests were being destroyed "by fire and axe". Every summer forest fires raged, filling the valley with smoke until snow fell and extinguished them, and timber companies indiscriminately cut timber wherever they pleased. The western Sierra Madre (Hayden) was established in 1906. The two were combined in 1985.

Forest management began and several forest rangers patrolled the thousands of acres on horseback, checking timber and grazing permits. Sheep and cattlemen had grazed their stock wherever they pleased since 1882, but had to take assignments and pay fees after 1905. Livestock, 18 thousand cattle and 50 thousand sheep, grazed in the forest in 1939.

The largest timber cut in history was 114 million board feet on 18 thousand acres at Douglas Creek (Keystone) in 1934.

The 1980's and 1990's were crazy, frightening times for the lumber industry. The power saw and mechanized logging of the 1970's had greatly improved production but had brought low prices for the finished product.

Environmental activism swept the nation, and these extreme groups gave no thought to jobs lost or the economy. They preached "natural" forest management and protested, appealed and brought lawsuits that delayed and hampered timber sales. The Forest Service reduced sales to 18 million board feet in 1985 from a previous 54 million board feet in 1975.

New regulations concerning air and water quality brought the lumber industry to its knees. When nine important sales weren't made, logging companies and workers moved to other jobs.

Hines Lumber Company (1968-1983), successor to the R.R. Crow mill in Saratoga, sold to Louisiana Pacific (1983-2003), who closed the mill. We all thought that our industry was gone forever, and the Forest Service had also lost its most important management tool. Mills had closed all over the country and none were left in Wyoming. The U.S. had to purchase building materials from Canada.

Mother Nature showed us that she was boss (1997-2012) when a spruce and pine beetle epidemic swept through the West, infesting mature and young lodgepole pines and turning them into grey skeletons.

The beetles were aided by drought conditions. We had suppressed and fought fires for a century, and the forest was unhealthy and dense. We know now that fire cleanses and rejuvenates, and the Forest Service has adopted controlled fire methods that use natural and man-made barriers to keep fires confined. Balanced management stresses preservation, sustainability and aesthetics.

Our lumber industry is back in business today, thanks to Gary Erwin who persisted in his quest for the Saratoga lumber mill. Saratoga Forest Management (2012-) employs 100 people and trucks carry Saratoga Straight 2x4's to markets. Air quality regulations closed the waste burner; trucks now take sawdust to playgrounds, and chips are sent to Walden and processed into chipboard. Shavings are used for mulch, animal bedding and pellets.

The Forest Service is presently on a five year plan that will produce 60 million board feet each year. Grazing of livestock has been radically reduced to make way for a burgeoning tourist industry.

TOURISM

From mountain crest to mountain crest this valley had been Indian hunting grounds for centuries.

Pizen Bill Hooker, an old freighter, described the country of the 1850's and 60's. He said there were "great herds of antelope and elk on the plains, prairie chickens by the hundreds and thousands of jack rabbits as plentiful as flies in the barnyard." John Mullison prospected here in the 1860's and said this was a hunting paradise.

Stories about the abundant wildlife circulated, and after the Utes were sent to their new Utah reservation and the valley was being settled, wealthy and aristocratic men came in the 1880's to hunt. Each arrived at Fort Steele with their entourage of friends and servants for two months of hunting. Local guides took them to Sweetwater country, the Platte Valley and into northern Colorado.

Display of elk heads, ca. 1900

When these hunters saw the large herds of animals they fired non-stop with their 18-cartridge Winchesters and ordered their hides, horns and heads to be shipped back home for trophies. Our Territorial Legislature was aghast at the carnage and passed game laws that restricted hunting only for food, and only two animals a day for each hunter. Shipping of wild meat to meat markets and shipping of animal hides and antlers were felonies. But enforcement of these laws was difficult until Wyoming Game and Fish was established.

Many meat-hungry people arrived in the 80's and 90's—prospectors, loggers, and miners. Locals also hunted for their families.

Elk were hunted out by 1910, so 100 head from Jackson Hole were transplanted in the Medicine Bows in 1912; they were held at Elk Hollow until spring when they were released. An additional 65 were transplanted in the Sierra Madres in 1915, and all elk hunting was closed until it was reopened on October 15, 1955. Antelope season was closed 1908 to 1927.

Elk for transplant were held at Elk Hollow.

A state game warden was appointed in 1899 which led to the formation of the Wyoming Game and Fish Commission in 1908. It is an independent and professional organization free of political influence.

The Game and Fish keeps animal counts, sets hunting boundaries and distributes licenses accordingly. A few Big Horn sheep are harvested each year near Encampment, and one or two moose that migrated here from Colorado are harvested. Solitary black bear roam the forest looking for people food. A few are harvested each year.

Bear in the street, ca. 1917

Baldy Sisson at the wheel and Charlie Plummer lying down in front of the Sisson Hotel after a day of mule deer hunting.

...

Fishing is phenomenal in the Upper North Platte Valley's "Blue Ribbon Trout Stream." But fish had not naturally evolved here. Two periods of mountain building, movement and much erosion had occurred when fish could have evolved. McPhee tells us that the river had established its channel only 1.6 million years ago.

Fish were accidentally planted in the early 1880's when a Union Pacific train carrying large cans of rainbow and brook fingerling trout was stalled at Fort Steele. Trainmen discovered that the fish were dying and they dumped the remaining fish into the North Platte River.

Ranchmen saw that the fish had taken kindly to their new home and began transplanting fish on their creeks. C.W. Scott caught a 2¾ pound fish near the Saratoga bridge in 1892 and a fishing frenzy began. Everyone soon had a fishing pole in hand and "Gone Fishing" signs were posted on doorways.

By 1900 it seemed that the supply of fish was inexhaustible and anglers came from far and wide to enjoy the sportiest fishing in the West. Large fish weighing eight or ten pounds were mounted and hung in picture frames for everyone to see. When the S&E railroad was built to Saratoga, 1,000 celebrants ate over 3,000 fish that had been caught in river tributaries. There were no limits on fish, and people made pigs of themselves

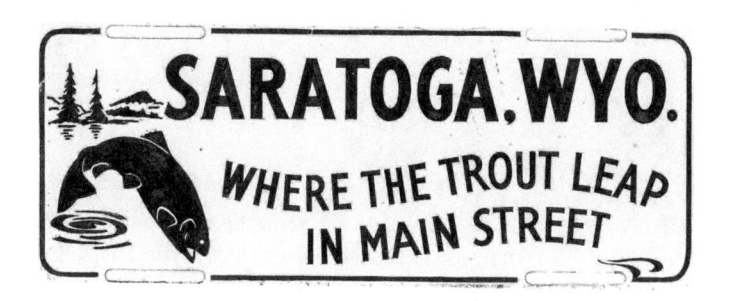

SARATOGA, WYO.
WHERE THE TROUT LEAP IN MAIN STREET

"Where the fish leap in Main Street" is Saratoga's earliest slogan. Billy O'Neil, a popular sportswriter, coined the phrase in 1927 when he visited here and was sitting on the east porch of the Sierra Madre Clubhouse when he saw fish rising in the river. Because the clubhouse was located on the river's edge at the head of Main Street he was inspired to title his article in the Outdoor Life magazine.

Baldy (George) Sisson was called "the world's champion trout fisherman" because he could catch fish when no one else could. When asked what bait he used, he replied, "It ain't the fly so much, you have to skitter him along the water."

Baldy and his wife Rhoda purchased Hotel Wolf in 1919. Baldy was best friend to the Wolf's deceased son Fred. The hotel was renamed the Sisson and it became known as "fishermen's headquarters" when the personable Baldy became a fishing guide for the patrons. Baldy and two hotel guests were drowned in

July, 1935 when his boat capsized in some deep, swift water below town.

Garrett Price, 10 years old, is in the center of this photo with Baldy Sisson. Price later became a world-renowned cartoonist and wrote in his memoire (housed at the the UW American Research Center) about his fishing experiences:
"Baldy sisson, called the 'World's Greatest Trout Fisherman" got a merciless kidding this particular day. I caught more trout than he."
"I once won a five dollar gold piece for the most fish caught for the fish fry." He caught 105 fish.

"IT'S A FINE PLACE TO STAY"

SISSON HOTEL
SARATOGA, WYOMING
J. EARLE MOORE, Proprietor

FISHING   HOT MINERAL SPRINGS   HUNTING   WINTER SPORTS

Float fishing began in 1903 on a small scale, but became more and more popular. Fred Bonfils of the Denver Post hosted yearly ten-day floats for his friends and associates; the floats began in July 1912 and continued until 1933. Bonfils purchased five sturdy wooden boats and stored the camp equipment in Saratoga. He hired W.C Large and five boatsmen. Two campmovers with a grubwagon and a hayrack carried supplies and camp equipment between river campsites. (There was a 20 fish limit per day back then.)

Fly fishing at Sheeprock, ca. 1915

Local "river rats" began guiding for hire, and before long float fishing became a popular sport. A bitter feud between floaters and ranchers festered and came to a head in 1958 when several ranchers on the river claimed ownership of the land and water that flowed through their lands.

Len Bensen was guide for Verg Teter's business in 1956-58.

He said that the all-day floats between Beaver Creek and Saratoga were very popular, but they passed by the river bank homes of John Rouse, Gene Rouse and Ken Day, and floaters used loud and foul language and had been seen naked. The boats stopped wherever they pleased to cook and eat their lunches and left their trash. The ranchers decided to stop trespassing; they strung wire across the river. Len was assigned to patrol ahead of the boats and cut the wire so boats could pass safely. A lawsuit followed.

Outfitters Len and Pat Bensen float fishing the Platte Rver, ca. 1970

The Wyoming Supreme Court settled the case in 1959: ranchers have ownership of shore land and the land beneath the water, but water is owned by the public. Therefore, floating the river is legal but boats should not stop except in emergency.

The Wyoming Game and Fish realized that river access points were needed and they bought river ranches, kept access land, and then sold the ranchlands. Hazardous white water floating on the upper waters requires experienced guides.

A wild trout management program was put into effect in 1984.

INDUSTRIES 87

UPPER NORTH PLATTE RIVER

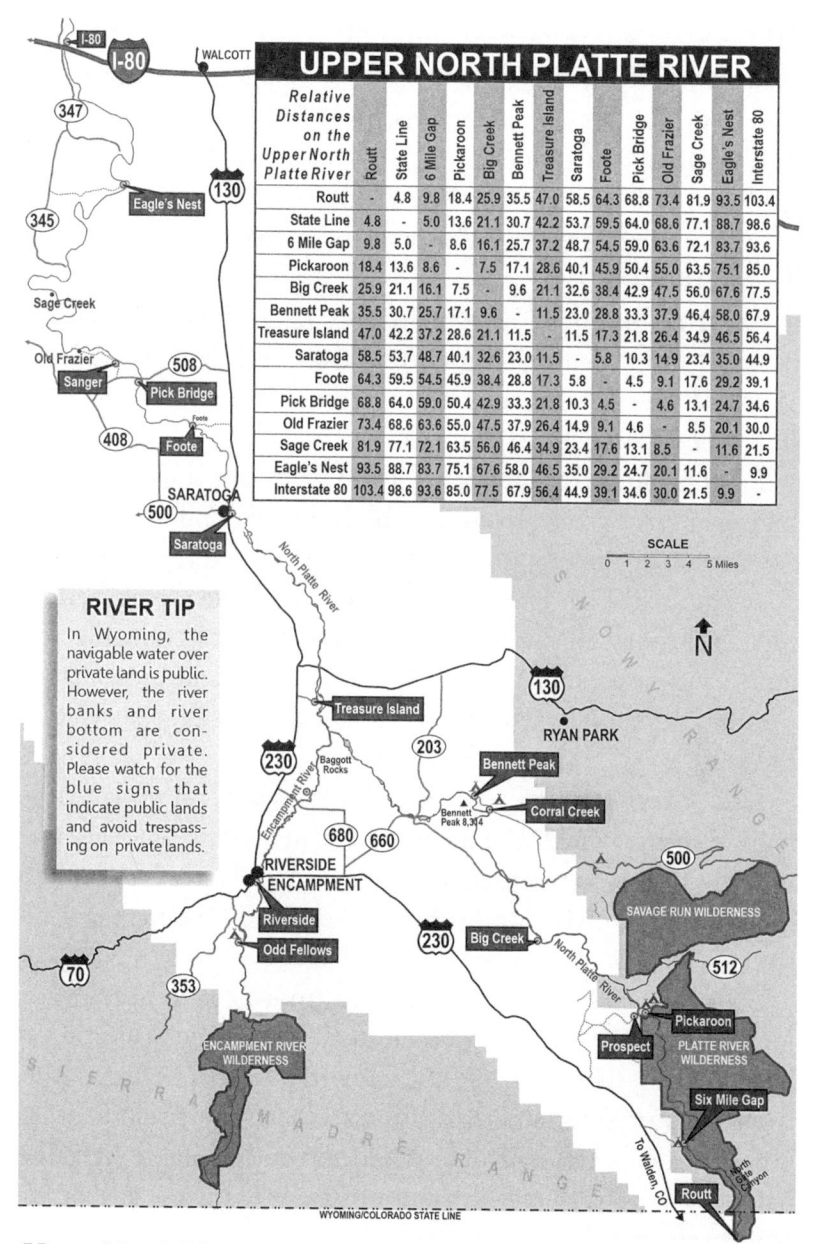

Relative Distances on the Upper North Platte River	Routt	State Line	6 Mile Gap	Pickaroon	Big Creek	Bennett Peak	Treasure Island	Saratoga	Foote	Pick Bridge	Old Frazier	Sage Creek	Eagle's Nest	Interstate 80
Routt	-	4.8	9.8	18.4	25.9	35.5	47.0	58.5	64.3	68.8	73.4	81.9	93.5	103.4
State Line	4.8	-	5.0	13.6	21.1	30.7	42.2	53.7	59.5	64.0	68.6	77.1	88.7	98.6
6 Mile Gap	9.8	5.0	-	8.6	16.1	25.7	37.2	48.7	54.5	59.0	63.6	72.1	83.7	93.6
Pickaroon	18.4	13.6	8.6	-	7.5	17.1	28.6	40.1	45.9	50.4	55.0	63.5	75.1	85.0
Big Creek	25.9	21.1	16.1	7.5	-	9.6	21.1	32.6	38.4	42.9	47.5	56.0	67.6	77.5
Bennett Peak	35.5	30.7	25.7	17.1	9.6	-	11.5	23.0	28.8	33.3	37.9	46.4	58.0	67.9
Treasure Island	47.0	42.2	37.2	28.6	21.1	11.5	-	11.5	17.3	21.8	26.4	34.9	46.5	56.4
Saratoga	58.5	53.7	48.7	40.1	32.6	23.0	11.5	-	5.8	10.3	14.9	23.4	35.0	44.9
Foote	64.3	59.5	54.5	45.9	38.4	28.8	17.3	5.8	-	4.5	9.1	17.6	29.2	39.1
Pick Bridge	68.8	64.0	59.0	50.4	42.9	33.3	21.8	10.3	4.5	-	4.6	13.1	24.7	34.6
Old Frazier	73.4	68.6	63.6	55.0	47.5	37.9	26.4	14.9	9.1	4.6	-	8.5	20.1	30.0
Sage Creek	81.9	77.1	72.1	63.5	56.0	46.4	34.9	23.4	17.6	13.1	8.5	-	11.6	21.5
Eagle's Nest	93.5	88.7	83.7	75.1	67.6	58.0	46.5	35.0	29.2	24.7	20.1	11.6	-	9.9
Interstate 80	103.4	98.6	93.6	85.0	77.5	67.9	56.4	44.9	39.1	34.6	30.0	21.5	9.9	-

RIVER TIP

In Wyoming, the navigable water over private land is public. However, the river banks and river bottom are considered private. Please watch for the blue signs that indicate public lands and avoid trespassing on private lands.

Upper North Platte River access points and relative float distances. Courtesy of Cindy Loose, VIP's Guide to Southern Wyoming.

Objectives were to protect larger fish, improve spawning and maintain a large population of fish per mile The first slot limits were 6 fish with only one over 16 inches; the present limits are 3 fish with one of 16 inches. "Catch and release" is the preferred fishing method today. The North Platte River, 65 miles from the Colorado line to Sage Creek, was designated a Blue Ribbon Trout Stream in 1987.

The Encampment River had only been floated in kayaks before 1995. Local fishing enthusiasts Sterling Arnold, Will Ward, Walter Freshman and Pat Homer conquered that river in a 14-foot rubber raft that year.

Float fishing is one of our most popular sports now. Camping, hiking and ATV travels also rate high. Snowmobiling and cross country skiing are popular winter sports, as well as ice fishing.

A National Fish Hatchery was built on Lake Creek, several miles northeast of Saratoga, in 1915; its work is valuable and unique; it ensures a large propagation of lake and brown trout throughout the United States. Not many fish eggs survive in the wild.

Lake Creek is only a few miles long; its water source is a large natural spring where the hatchery is located. After hatchery use, water impurities are settled in a pond and the water is sent on to Lake Creek, which empties into Silver Sage Ranch's beautiful river meadows.

Fish culturists assemble on Monday mornings to select ready females from the hatchery's broad stock; their spawn is fertilized by male milt, then carefully stirred with a feather. After a time, when eggs are determined disease-free, the eggs are sent to other hatcheries where the fish are raised to transplantable size. The hatchery originally raised fish and stocked streams and lakes, but it only spawns and fertilizes eggs now.

...

The cold blooded murder of two game wardens occurred on Halloween, October 31, 1945. They were shot west of the Continental Divide on Nuggett Gulch, east of Tullis and High Savery Reservoir. It was one of the most chilling and controversial events in Carbon County history.

Head game warden Bill Lakanen of Rawlins and assistant Don Simpson of Saratoga set out that morning to check on German alien John Malden who was known to have trapped beaver illegally. He had been arrested in November 1943 for unlicensed possession of 88 beaver pelts, 88 trout and deer meat and had served six months in the Carbon County jail, with one month added because he could not pay the $100.00 fine. October through March were prime beaver trapping months and the game wardens needed to make the difficult trip before winter set in.

John Maden cabin, ca. 1943

Their pickup pulled up to the Malden cabin, and before Lakanen could step out, he was shot through the head. Simpson attempted to reach cover in the nearby woods, but was also shot.

Their bodies and a burned cabin were discovered by a neighboring rancher several days later. A foot of snow blanketed the area. Three law officers came on November 3rd to investigate and retrieve the bodies.

But where was John Malden? Therein was the controversy. His automobiles were still there. Had he committed suicide and been cremated in the burning cabin? Or had he walked away to an unknown destination?

Examination of the cabin's ashes revealed a few bones of possible human origin and the charred high power .22 rifle that a neighbor had given Malden for protection from bears. (Malden was a felon and could not purchase a gun.) Present research indicates that the fire was not hot enough to cremate Malden. A 1300-1600 degree temperature for three hours is required. On the chance that Malden had walked away, the law searched the west range down to Grand Junction, but they were unable to find any hint of his presence there.

There had been talk during World War II that Malden had been a sharp shooter in the Kaiser's army, and that he was a German sympathizer and a spy—he had a short wave radio with a strong antenna that could reach Germany.

We do know that he was age 55, five-foot-ten inches tall, weighed around 200 pounds and was "strong as a bull." He had settled in Chicago after coming to the U.S. and had married. He came west after his wife died and became a gardener for Edgar Uihlien, a wealthy Schlitz brewer from Chicago, who had purchased the Brush Creek Ranch in 1925 and sold it in 1948. During his ownership trees and shrubbery were planted, and a large home was built with a beautiful rock garden over the slope below it. We don't know Malden's exact role in that development.

CHAPTER SIX

Changes

TRANSPORTATION

It has taken over 100 years to make the transition from horse and buggy travel until now, when we regularly make a trip to Rawlins, Laramie or Cheyenne in our all-wheel vehicles and think little of it.

Automobiles appeared on our roads in 1913. People of means promptly purchased them, then quickly discovered that two-track roads through the sagebrush were not very accommodating and that they knew little about auto mechanics and service.

A common occurrence in those days when horses became acquainted with the sight, sound and smell of the new automobile was described by Paul Breniman: As he was driving his team down Cedar Creek road one day he saw a cloud of dust and heard the sound of a motor in the distance. He quickly turned his horses as far as he could off the road, got out of his wagon and firmly held the horse bridles until the car had passed. On Saratoga's streets horses tore away from hitching rails when an automobile approached.

By 1920 there were 21,000 automobiles in Wyoming, but there were only 100 miles of graveled roads, and building roads and highways was expensive. The problem was solved by taxing automobiles and selling car and driving licenses. Royalties from the new gas and oil industry also helped. The Parco/Sinclair oil refinery was built in 1925.

Good Roads Day was proclaimed in 1920. Ranchers took the day off to grade roads and build culverts and bridges. It would be several decades before country roads were raised, graveled and cattle guards installed. Folks often said that it took more time to open and close gates between ranch properties than actual travel time. Four-wheel drive vehicles gradually became available after World War II.

The new automobile brought out the wanderlust in people, but there was so much to learn about the care and operation of the new invention. Three garages with gas dispensers opened on Saratoga's Bridge Street in 1919—the Wyoming, Central and River Street. The first filling station opened east of the bridge in 1925; it opened in conjunction with the Gould Cottage Camp—our first motel.

The new River Street Garage and old Hugus store front with Model T's, ca. 1920

CHANGES 93

First filling station - 314 E. Bridge Ave., ca. 1934

Model T Fords are parked on Bridge Avenue in this 1925 photo. Buildings left to right are Central Garage and Swifts Pool (which was moved later to the Wolf Annex). The Stockgrowers Bank (1919-1926), the Post Office (1920-1964) and the Ross Pharmacy are in the Burdick-Chatterton brick block (1892-present).

The dream of American adventurers was to travel across the country to see places they had never seen. Transcontinental Highway 30 was hastily roughed in and hardly navigable in 1915. There were no signs or maps, and makeshift wooden bridges crossed ravines. The Sun reported that Earl Scott's Kissell Kar truck had been stuck in one of the mud holes west of Medicine Bow for 14 hours. The highway had been built by horsepower but by 1934 with power machinery, more than half of Wyoming's highways had been raised and oiled, and cars could zip along at 25 mph. Service stations were built 20 miles apart, and cottage camps dotted the nation. By 1943 the Walcott-Encampment highway was oiled and cars could travel at a higher speed.

Our beloved Highway #130 crosses the Snowy Range in the Medicine Bow Mountains to Laramie. Twenty teams of horses constructed the highway on an old wagon road. Cars first drove the road when it was dedicated on July 4, 1926. It has since been widened and improved and was second in the nation to receive National Scenic Byway status.

First autos on the Snowy Range Highway, 1926

Dedication of Snowy Range Road in 1926.
Photo courtesy of Meyers Studio

Snowy Range was named by Laramie citizens, who noticed a high and snowy-looking ridge on the distant western horizon as they drove toward it. On examination they found that it was a five-mile white quartzite formation. (Quartztite is melted sea sand, billions of years old. It is called quartzite after it is melted with granite.) It was thrust upward to its 12,000 feet above sea level during mountain building periods. It is a natural wonder that overlooks Lake Marie and Mirror Lake and is called Medicine Bow Peak.

(Geologists theorize that American's high western mountain ranges were formed when continents were forming. The pushing and rubbing of continental plates caused the rise of mountains.)

The worst disaster in aviation history was reported by the Saratoga Sun on October 6, 1955. A United Airline passenger plane with 65 people aboard had crashed that morning on the east side of Medicine Bow Peak's quartzite cliff, a half mile north of Lake Marie. All of the people perished. It was believed that the pilot had attempted to make up lost time by making a shortcut and poor visibility contributed to the crash.

View of Lake Marie and Mirror Lake below Medicine Bow Peak, with the Sierra Madre Mountain Range in the distance. Photo courtesy of Cindy Loose.

Interstate 80 opened in October 1970. Trucking had greatly increased. Although local residents had warned engineers that the road they had chosen between Laramie and Walcott was ill-chosen, the engineers insisted on the more direct route. The fury of Wyoming winters was discovered the first winter when there were 151 accidents and the road was often closed. Locals named it the Sno Chi Minh Trail after the cruel leader of North Vietnam, Ho Chi Minh.

Engineers created a series of snow fences to alleviate the blowing snow. Summer tourists asked what these strange wood structures along Highway 80 were and were often told, "Why, they are wildlife viewing stands."

Battle Highway #70, a popular summer scenic byway leaves Encampment and crosses the Continental Divide to Savery and Baggs. In the winter we often cross at Walcott to old Highway 30 and pass Medicine Bow on our way to Laramie. We can also take Highway #230 past the Colorado state line to Laramie.

SHIVELY FIELD

Saratoga's airport was officially named Shively Field in August, 1952. It was dedicated to the memory of Lieutenant Jack E. Shively, who was killed on June 14, 1944 when his P51 Mustang was shot down over Chinon, France during World War II.

While flying with 20 other fighter bombers on a mission to destroy bridges, Shively dropped his plane—he was looking for a way to avoid unnecessary collateral damage. In the 8 o'clock evening sun he did not see four German Focke Wulfs high and hiding in the sun. One plane attacked, and Shively's plane exploded in mid-air. Shively is honored in Chinon for his sacrifice.

Jack Shively was the son of Ed and Pearl Shively and a favorite son to Saratoga.

Shively Field is one of the three largest airfields in Wyoming. Its story began in 1934, not long after the beginning of air flight.

The Lions Club began squabbling about the need for an airport in the late 1920's. When small planes and the Chicago-San

Lt. Jack Shively, WWII pilot

Francisco air mail planes (1920) were flying their routes over the Union Pacific railroad tracks, they occasionally encountered weather, altitude or plane difficulties and flew here for help. They often encountered dangerous ditches, barbwire fences and other impediments when they tried to land.

The town took hold of the airport project in 1934 when S.S. Sharp was mayor. He became engineer for the project with workers and funds available through the New Deal's WPA depression project. The town owned the perfect airfield land on a large flat on the bench south of town. Sagebrush was grubbed, land was leveled, and runways were set into the prevailing southwest winds.

First jet lands at Shively Field, one of Wyoming's best airports, ca. 1968

L.D. Donelan, Saratoga's new pharmacist, volunteered his help in 1935. He had acquired an affinity for flying while watching "barnstorming" antics during his Kansas boyhood. He spent his spare time picking up the many rocks that nicked propeller blades and eliminated gophers. Don met planes, provided taxi service, promoted the valley, and made friends. He hand-pumped fuel, set landing lights and supervised other improvements. Donelan was volunteer airport manager from 1945 to 1974, and it was largely due to his persistence that the airport proved itself and began receiving large grants and donations.

The first quarter mile runway grew to 8,800 feet by 1995, and airplane patronage has grown from eighty-seven planes in 1952 to several thousand planes, 99% of them jets, in 2017. Land, fences, parking, ramps, taxiways, lights and hangars have been added throughout the years. Tarmac was replaced in 2018.

The airport has been professionally run since 1974 by Welton Flying Service, Saratoga Aviation (1981-2018), and Mountain Flight Service (2018-present).

This area, with its cool, dry summers and its mountains and streams teeming with wildlife and fish, were a natural magnet. As private airplane ownership increased, business at Saratoga's airport increased.

Bill and Pic Walker, owners of a Cheyenne aviation service flew in and took note of the hot springs and the valley. They leased the hot springs property from the State and built the Saratoga Inn and golf course.

One of their guests, George B. Storer, who was an eastern broadcasting tycoon, tried to buy the Inn but was turned down. Determined to build his own resort, he found land on a high sagebrush hill overlooking the North Platte River and near the town and its airport. To the east a large, beautiful mountain with a bald peak rose. Locals always called it Old Baldy, but it had been renamed Kennaday Peak. Old Baldy would be the name of his exclusive member-owned new club that opened around 1964. The club and its members have been good, supportive friends to Saratoga and have given many employment opportunities to residents.

A.D. Davis from Florida purchased ranch properties in the 1960's. He and George Storer were the first large donors to our airport, which was attracting valley investors. Today, owners of large ranches—the TA, Overland Trail and Silver Spur—fly in. The Conquistadors del Cielo, a fraternity of aviation executives, fly in each September for their annual meeting at the A Bar A ranch, an old exclusive resort near Encampment.

Brush Creek Ranch (2009-present) owns a large jet that lands and takes off regularly at Shively Field. Brush Creek is a high-end, trendy resort with guests that require privacy and anonymity. It continues to expand its holdings and innovate with new projects. In 2014, Conde' Nast, a leading luxury travel magazine, announced its' Readers' Choice award. Brush Creek Ranch was selected the world's number two destination and number one in the United States.

John Malone, who loves rural land and wide open spaces, became owner of the original Silver Spur Ranch in 1999 and it has greatly expanded since then. But it is primarily a working cattle ranch with a smaller portion given to fishing and hunting guests.

SARATOGA HOT SPRINGS

The State Bath House (presently the property of the Saratoga Hot Springs Resort) and three cottages were built to accomodate bath house guests (one remains).

The celebrated Saratoga Hot Pool was discovered and developed in 1931. This was S.S. Sharp's last State Hot Springs project. The State Bathhouse had ceremoniously opened the year before and the park was finished.

A small hot pool was perched precariously on a hill on the southwest corner of the hot springs property. Vivian Jones said she went there occasionally to bathe. Three or four people could relax in the hot tub sized pool and enjoy the scenery.

But the hillside had fallen into the river in the late 1920's, and the spring was lying several feet from the riverbank. Sharp built concrete walls and measured the flow at 350,000 gallons of water a day. It flows at 450,000 a day now.

Hobo Hot Pool, ca. 1936

The CCC's rocked in the main spring, built rock steps and a log banister—a beautiful site that is still recognizable. Locals called it the Hobo Pool for many years when poor, foot-weary hoboes tramped the country looking for work; they found a welcome hot bath and a place to rest here.

The Town leased the hot pool and the island from the state for many years. They were able to purchase the properties in 1984, but the State stipulated that the pool must remain free and open to the public. Improvements, upkeep and meeting health safety and moral standards have been a costly and time-consuming challenge.

The CCC, with native timber and rocks they had cut and gathered, built benches, tables, a large shelter house with two fireplaces, and bridges. This picture shows the bridge they built to Cadwell-Veterans island at the same place where today's bridge is located.

A large municipal swimming pool opened in June 1958; youngsters receive important swimming lessons there each summer. There have been many valuable improvements throughout the year—walkways, fences, moss rock beautification, dressing rooms and showers and a large parking lot.

A recent addition is the Not So Hot Pool. The water measures 103 degrees and is very popular. The original enclosed Lobster Pot measures 120 degrees, and the larger pool is several degrees lower.

Saratoga Municipal Pool with Saratoga Inn and railroad tressel in background, ca. 1958

The hot springs are immensely popular with the parking lot full—especially in the summer. They are magical and therapeutic, but also a friendly social gathering place.

(The Saratoga Inn/Saratoga Resort has an interesting adaptation of the Indian Bathtubs for their guests to enjoy.)

HOT MINERAL SPRINGS

Hot mineral springs have been revered by man for their medicinal and spiritual qualities for ages.

The National Geographic recently published a hot spring edition stating that there are only about one thousand sites in the world where they are found, mainly in China, Japan, New Zealand, Canada and the United States. Wyoming's Yellowstone National park is the largest and most famous worldwide.

Wyoming, Colorado and Arkansas are the U.S. states that have major hot springs. (Saratoga Springs, New York's springs are cold.) Glenwood Springs in Colorado are the largest in the United States, aside from Yellowstone. Colorado has about thirty sites, some primitive; nearly all of them lie on the southwestern slope of the Rockies. Wyoming's other major springs, aside from Saratoga's, are at Thermopolis.

Before modern medicines and treatments, hot mineral springs offered people their only relief from arthritis and joint pains. When they drank the water it helped digestive ailments.

VETERANS ISLAND

Veterans Island has held a special place in our hearts for nearly 150 years. It was once part of William Cadwell's hot spring property and was called Cadwell's Island.

Early settlers discovered it was a fine gathering place, with shade trees and protection from the wind. Before the iron bridge was built in 1885, they crossed the two river channels to the Cadwell store to get their mail and purchase supplies.

The Fourth of July was a special time, with patriotic oratory. They ate and socialized, then danced the night away while Chinese lanterns hung from tree branches. Drinking or rowdy behavior was not tolerated.

Saratoga's famous fish fries were held there from 1907 to 1915. It has been the place to go for other large events: the Nation's Bicentennial, Saratoga's 75th birthday, small and large class reunions and many other events.

The Town leased the island and hot springs in the 1920's and after much effort and persuasion was able to purchase them in 1984. Countless volunteer hours and large amounts of money have been spent in upkeep and improvements.

Bank stabilization started in 1999 when the river began tearing at the upper tip and south bank. The floods of 2010-2011 caused much concern. The river is temperamental and wants more room but is confined to a narrow channel. It rampages past Veterans Island, then spreads out between the two bridges and dumps its river rock. This is a continuous problem that has not been solved.

Lions at Veterans Island, ca. 1950's

WORLD WAR I (1914-1918)

Europe was in a state of change which brought about World War I. The European nations after centuries of serfdoms and caste systems were ruled by hereditary dynasties who knew little about compromise or diplomacy.

The Russian Czar and the German Kaiser touched off the war in June 1914 and soon other nations were involved—they declared war on each other or chose sides with Russia or Germany.

The U.S. had two democratic allies, Britain and France, and was determined to help by providing food and supplies. With patriotic fervor, our people observed meatless Tuesdays, flourless days and took the sugar bowls off the table. Gone also were midnight feeds and afternoon teas. When they saw allied forces faltering, the U.S. declared war on Germany on April 5, 1917, and promptly drafted two million men, age 21 to 31.

After marching for hours through rain and mud to the front, they discovered a new kind of warfare—large machine guns that fired 600 cartridges every minute, massive artillery and a mustard gas that burned through clothing and flesh. Gas masks and deep trenches were their only defense.

The U.S. and Britain developed one-man machine guns and armored tanks, and they took more ground in four hours than they had in the previous four months while the new aeroplanes observed from the skies.

Germany signed an unconditional surrender on November 11, 1918. Everyone thought this was the war to end all wars. The U.S. was recognized as a world leader after its war leadership assistance. A great patriotism and "can do" attitude developed in our country.

The Spanish Flu was brought home by returning soldiers. It ravished the world and killed a half million U.S. citizens, 150 in

Carbon County, 4 in Saratoga.

War veterans chartered the Angus England American Legion Post 54 on November 2, 1921. It was named for Angus England, a favorite son descended from the Campbell ranchers on Pass Creek. He was killed in the Battle of Argonne in the final days of the war. The Legion keeps patriotism alive by leading parades, observing Armistice Day and teaching patriotism. The women's Auxiliary was organized in 1927. These organizations have been a valuable asset to Saratoga.

Angus England

"THE ROARING TWENTIES"

This was a time that transformed our culture and attitudes. Victorian restrictions were put aside. The economy surged. People were fascinated by the new automobiles which the common man could at last afford to buy.

The austerity and frugality of World War I had produced the 18th Amendment which prohibited the sale and use of alcoholic beverages in 1918. The 19th Amendment in 1919 gave women the right to vote.

In response, women threw away their tight girdles, bobbed their long hair and shortened their skirts. It was the age of the "fliver and the flapper" and "moonshine" whiskey—a time of irresistible and naughty challenge.

It was easy to illegally make moonshine, and some men were willing to take the risk because it was a profitable business. "Stills" had to be moved often or the law would find and destroy them. Selling was tricky, too. Some bootleggers were careless and produced bad whiskey that could blind or kill, so buyers soon learned to purchase from reputable bootleggers.

Paul Breniman said that saloons became speakeasies and pool halls, and cigar stores and brothels became places where alcohol was secretly served in tall glasses with ice and ginger ale. If the marshal walked in, drinks were quickly gathered and dumped.

Paul recalled dances at the Amos Wilcox dance pavilion (the Flying Diamond Ranch). He would take a carload of friends there, well-armed with "hootch", or to the Medicine Bow Lodge's yearly opening dance. He said, "Good girls didn't drink, but a few did and they were really fun."

John V. was a memorable bootlegger. He drove a fancy, high powered car, often accompanied by a woman, and he could outrun any lawman. Georgia Ward said that when her husband was marshal, the town couldn't afford a car; he walked his rounds, checking for locked doors and peeking through windows of businesses that he suspected were serving illicit liquor.

The county sheriff raided one year and caught the Ferris Haggarty Hotel in the act. They were closed down and the ladies were sent out of town. The Waterloo's second story was another well-known hangout where a piano player furnished music for patrons until the wee hours.

In 1928 S.S. Sharp brought in Otto Plaga to help catch bootleggers. Plaga had been a successful federal prohibition officer; he had destroyed many stills and hundreds of mash barrels, kegs of booze, thousands of gallons of whiskey, and beer and wine in eastern Wyoming. Plaga was a wiry, black-haired, ex-rodeo cowboy who had a memorable ride on Steamboat, king of bucking horses. Plaga was able to rake Steamboat's sides with his spurs and had survived 88 jumps before he was thrown.

The government realized that it could not enforce the 18th Amendment and repealed it in 1938. Because Wyoming needed legislative action, our folks couldn't drink legally until April 1, 1934. The Wyoming Liquor Commission was established then; all liquor is sold and taxes collected by them. Towns were allowed one liquor license per 500 population. Saratoga, with a population of 600, got two. The town was paid $500.00 for each license.

Tex Corpening spent his boyhood in Saratoga, and his young eyes and ears took everything in. He said, "There was lots of gambling with high stakes at Swift's Pool Hall. Stakes ran as high as several thousand dollars. If you learned to gamble in Saratoga, you could hold your own anyplace."

An anti-gambling law had been passed in 1904 by the State, but nearly every town in the state had open gambling, said Dr. Roy Wilson, town dentist. "The towns would simply fine the gambling establishments and the gambling would continue." The fines kept the towns running; money was scarce in the days before sales tax and federal monies were available.

> "Lots of people came here to gamble," said Georgia Ward, whose family came here in 1925. "Gambling was wide open and consisted of poker, a roulette wheel, a crap table and lots of slot machines."

> Don Henderson came here to search for work in 1933. He said, "There were big crowds in town. It was a lively place with lots of fights. If you wanted excitement, you didn't have to leave Saratoga."

Bob and Mary Martin were owner publishers of the Saratoga Sun (1944-1968). Bob's father had purchased the Sun in 1917.

Both men were extraordinarily interested in local history and articles in the Sun reflected their interest.

Bob Martin gathered history and photographs from valley old timers and planned to write a local history book. But his health failed and he asked his protege Dick Perue to care for and make use of his sixty box collection.

Perue has faithfully done this. He has added lots more to the Martin collection, known today as the Martin-Perue Historical Photograph Collection. Dick was editor of the Saratoga Sun (1958-1974); he purchased the printing and newspaper business in 1968 and sold it in 1982.

Robert D. and Mary Martin, ca. 1926, author's collection. Bob formed and led The Novelty Dance Band, which played through the 1920's and 1930's. The band often played until dawn, when it was safe for the dancers to go home in their Model A's and T's on the early roads.

"THE THRIFTY THIRTIES"

Have you ever sat by a wood stove and listened to the radio while your mother darned socks and mended and patched clothes? Have you seen your father straighten nails and half-sole shoes? Worn a beautiful green wool coat made from an aunt's old coat that had been taken apart and the fabric turned, cut and sewn? Slept under a wool patch quilt? Heard the expression, "A penny saved is a dollar earned"? If so, you never forgot it.

The nation's stock market crashed on Black Thursday, October 24, 1929. After a decade of high living it was a shock. There had been warnings and banks closed in the 1920's—they had been under-capitalized and under-regulated. Perhaps people should have followed the old adage: "If it's too good to be true, it's probably not true."

President Hoover, in his March 4, 1929 inaugural address, said the country was at its zenith with corporate leadership and new technology. But within three years the economy had collapsed and the middle class had been wiped out. Savings were gone, and over one third of the work force had lost their jobs.

Howard Corpening described the times:

> "The wrath of god was cast upon the land in 1929. The security market broke, resulting in a domino effect that brought the entire economy to a standstill—a land of disaster. Then the drought hit; ranchers were harvesting tumble weeds and cattle were starving.
>
> "People were four years behind on taxes and interest, with no possible way of raising a dime. Most ranchers did not lack from food and shelter, and could barter with cream, milk and meat to obtain necessities.
>
> "At this time few people known to me paid any income

tax, there being a four thousand dollar exemption, which was considered quite a lot of money in those days."

Franklin Delano Roosevelt took office in 1933. He calmly and reassuringly told the America people in his radio "fireside chats" that we have nothing to fear except fear itself, and went to work. Government salaries were reduced; relief funds went to the states for the hungry and unemployed.

The Civilian Conservation Corps was immediately started; it was part of the National Recovery Act and was funded with $3.3 billion for public works. The Social Security Act was passed, labor unions were allowed, and a two-cent sales tax went into effect.

The CCC arrived here in 1934. One camp of 200 young men built their camp east of town within the stone gateway next to the fairgrounds. Another camp was built near Ryan Park. The CCC employed young men, age 17 through 23, from needy families and paid them $30.00 a month, with $25.00 sent back home. The CCC was dedicated to building men through education, religion and athletics.

Civilian Conservation Corps. camp east of town, ca. 1936. Presently the new Saratoga Inn Overlook Subdivision.

They performed many worthwhile and lasting public works. During their six years here they improved Wyoming's hot springs property and the hot pool, and they built campgrounds, bridges and fences in the national parks. The Brush Creek Ranger station and the main ranger office (212 S. River Street) were built in 1938.

CCC boys at Saratoga camp

The town swelled with these handsome young men who competed with local lads for the affections of our young ladies. Soda fountains, Firemen's Hall dances, and the recently remodeled Legion Theater were popular gathering places. The new Hobo Hot Springs were enjoyed in the afterhours by the young men.

The human spirit was very much alive in the tough days of the depression. When hobos came to the door searching for odd jobs and a meal, they were fed, often with a sandwich. Sliced bread was sold for five cents a loaf after 1930—hence the expression "the greatest thing since sliced bread." Mrs. Walker, a widow with three children, baked bread for a living; her children worked whenever possible and learned thrift, good work habits and the satisfaction of a job well done.

Humor dispelled gloom. Butch Turnbull in earlier tough times was a town character always full of spirit. He invented nicknames for freighters: Alkali Ike, Baling Wire Jake, and G-String Jack. Gus Jensen had a scarred face and was called Chief Rain-in-the-face. Bible-back Nixon, Buffalo Charlie who had shot Bill Cadwell's pet buffalo, and café owner Dough Knuckle Bill were other nicknames.

April Fools and Halloween pranks were imaginative and fun to talk and laugh about. Families listened to wonderful comedians on the radio—George Burns, Jack Benny, and Edgar Bergen among others. Families played cards and games with friends and neighbors.

Frances Hughes moved here in 1935 and worked as a waitress in one of the cafes. She lived in a boarding house with other young people and wrote about some of the shenanigans of the depression years.

The young people often gathered in one of their rooms in the evenings to laugh and talk. One night a young gentleman sat on her bed and took off his shoes. He went back to his room and forgot to take his shoes. In the morning he came back to get his shoes and was caught carrying them from her room. It was the hilarious talk of the town for a few days.

People couldn't afford weddings in those days and just quietly got married. But they were chivareed by friends who gathered together and made loud noises and banged on the newlywed's door until they were let in. Frances and Frank Hughes refused to let them in, so a young man climbed to the roof and covered the chimney with his coat. The smoke drove them out. Sometimes the groom had to push his bride in a wheelbarrow through town.

Around 1935 a young babysitter was seen crossing Preach Campbell's lawn in the middle of the night, and he was fired from the Presbyterian Church pulpit. He bought the Legion Theater and showed movies at night, and he successfully started his Community Church and the popular youth group called the

Christian Endeavor.

The town's womenfolk were put into a frenzy when word got out that there was a peeping tom. They were very careful to cover every window peephole after that.

There was not much said out loud in the 1940's when a town councilman's wife caught him leaving the covered stairs that led to Kay's place in the upper story of Swift's Pool Hall. The angry wife rushed to the Town Hall and demanded that Kay be sent out of town immediately. She and her one-arm pimp were gone the next day. This ended many years of prostitution in the town.

WORLD WAR II (1941-1945), KOREA, VIETNAM

Germany was worn out, deeply in debt and hopeless after its defeat in World War I. It was fertile ground for Adolph Hitler, a fast-talking man who preached Germany's return to glory and a philosophy of Arian-pure Nordic white-supremacy. He was elected chancellor in 1933 but quickly became an evil dictator. Freedoms of speech and the press disappeared, but people were happy when jobs became available. They did not understand when objectors and their Jewish neighbors were taken away by train to unknown destinations.

The massive Nazi war machine began taking over neighboring countries in the late 1930's and was allied with Mussolini, dictator of Italy. The U.S. could foresee war in 1940 and began military buildup and the draft.

A new danger lurked in the Pacific. Japan, in a quest for land and markets, had occupied Manchuria, Korea and Taiwan in the 1930's; possession of the stepping stone islands in the Pacific was their next goal; they bombed U.S. naval ships at Pearl Harbor, Hawaii on December 7, 1941.

World War II had begun, and the U.S. was at war in the Pacific, as well as across the Atlantic. It quickly mobilized and called for a massive scrap iron drive so armaments, ships and planes could be built.

WWII scrap metal drive, ca. 1942

The valley CCC camps were drafted, as well as our younger men. Citizens patriotically bought war savings bonds, submitted to food rationing and shortage of gas, rubber tires and other items. Red Cross ladies knitted, baked and raised money for the cause. Flags with stars appeared on windows—blue for sons who were serving, and gold for those who were killed.

There was a labor shortage, so women worked in war plants, on ranches, farms, and gas stations to make up for the labor shortage. Some women joined the women armed forces. They helped win the war.

Italian and German prisoners of war were housed at former CCC camps to work in the timber.

Cars, tires, refrigerators and clothes washers were not manufactured, and speed limits were fixed at 35 miles per hour to save on gas.

We won the war. Victory in Europe (VE Day) was announced on May 8, 1945 and Victory over Japan (VJ Day) in August.

The cruelty of Hitler's regime was found after the war. The people shipped from their homeland had been shot, worked and starved to death in labor camps, and several million were gassed in what they had believed were showers. Their bodies were buried in mass graves or incinerated.

The Japanese had retreated to their home islands in mid-1945. The U.S. realized that it would be a long and costly battle to defeat them on their home turf.

We had developed the atomic bomb and had tested it. It was a terrible weapon. Should we use it? Harry Truman, our commander in chief decided. Yes! Most people approved.

On August 6, 1945, two planes each carrying a bomb, sped two days apart to bomb Hiroshima and Nagasaki. The world was chilled by the devastating results!

Our servicemen came home from the war; many went to college on the GI bill. They got married and produced the baby boom generation. There was also a building boom and high employment. A strong economy prevailed for several decades. These times have often been described as some of the best in our history and a strong middle class emerged.

Memorial Day, ca. 1948. This space is now the modern River Street Garage with parking lot.

Soon after World War II ended, The "Cold War" descended. It was a race for atomic weapons, but also a question of Communist communal sharing versus Democratic capitalism. The Soviet Union, once a world power, was bent upon world domination with Communist China also involved.

Wars had been fought in Korea and Vietnam, and each was divided into north and south sections—the upper portion held by the Communists.

The Korean War (1952-1953) was a blood bath with nothing gained. We lost 36,000 men with 100,000 missing or wounded in a 16-month period.

Bill Schroeder's Vietnam War story is only representative of the thousands of stories that could be told, but most of our heroic veterans are reluctant to tell of their harrowing and death-filled experiences that left many mentally or physically crippled for life. We honor and thank them.

Schroeder was drafted into the Marines in 1965 and served two tours (1966-1968) on missions to prevent Viet Cong incursion from the north. He was squad leader for 9 to 14 men. "Good guys," he said.

The assigned area was comprised of Viet Cong farm villages, rice paddies and brush hills. In the winter, heavy rains called monsoons were common. The squad carried heavy packs filled with gear, ammo and C-rations. M14s, machine guns, and bazookas that shot flares into the air at night were their fighting equipment. Attacks could occur at any time, so the men slept only in 10-minute "snatches". Booby traps — hand grenades in tin cans — could be anywhere.

The squad was on duty for months. They communicated with base by radio. Only if a man was sick or injured was he taken by helicopter to base. The helicopter also dropped off supplies. On Schroeder's last tour they had an excellent sniffing scout dog, and his squad found an underground tunnel that protected them from surprise attacks at night.

Schroeder never regretted his tours in Vietnam and he felt some soldiers had a much rougher time. He went to college on the GI bill, received his accounting degree in three years and was Saratoga Town Treasurer for years.

Nearly three million men served their country during the Vietnam War. There were 58,000 deaths and 300,000 wounded, many with missing limbs and PTSD. It was a devisive war and the returning soldiers were not given the recognition and praise that they deserved. They all had their own varied and frightening experiences in Vietnam and in Iraq, Afghanistan and other places. WE THANK THEM ALL FOR THEIR SERVICE!

The end of World War II brought a truly miraculous transformation to the rural areas in America.

The Rural Electrification Association had been formed in 1935, but the war held up progress. Carbon Power and Light had been organized in February 1941 with nine rural board members from Saratoga, Encampment, Walcott and Elk Mountain, who planned on bringing electricity to the area by 1942.

When the war was over in 1945, work on lines began that were completed on August 10, 1948, when electric current flowed from Seminoe Dam to ranch homes.

Maude Wenonah Willford (1881-1977), local author and ranch wife, won a prize from Country Gentlemen magazine for her "My Day" essay. It is quoted here:

> "Here was the magic of Alladin—a dream come true! Light shone where lights had never been, the electric stove radiated heat, the washer turned, the mixer mixed, the corn popper popped—all the new appliances, ready for service, functioning by the turning of a switch.
>
> "I gazed, almost in disbelief upon the kitchen sink, complete with hot and cold water faucets and drain, and drew a mental picture of the stacks of dishes at shearing and haying time. The old hand pump is buried under six feet of snow. Let it stay there! Gone is the bucket that sat on the bench. The hated slop bucket is no more.
>
> "Goodbye Old Toilet on the Hill! Here is a title for a song. I could perch in my new bathroom and sing that song in glee.
>
> "I could review the strenuous and often amusing incidents of the days before REA came and secretly be glad that we had been tempered by the hard, lean years in preparation to appreciate and to enjoy new blessing of progress and prosperity."

Country roads were raised and graveled. Most ranch children attended the Saratoga school; a neighbor often drove area children to school and 14 year olds could drive, but only to and from school. A few Jeeps appeared after World War II, and by the 1970's four-wheel drives were common. With highways paved it became fairly common to drive to Rawlins for business and shopping for dress clothes or things we could not buy in Saratoga.

Saratoga State Park, R. R. Crow & Co. sawmill and Veterans Island, left center, in early 1940s.

There were four grocery stores here—small ones that carried basics and one size, one brand cans, and fresh fruits and vegetables only in season. Refrigerated trucks gradually began bringing in food from faraway places. No one had heard of packaged, ready-to-cook foods.

Fundraising for towers that would bring television to the valley began in 1956, and in October 1959 we sat before a black and white television set, at first not just snowy but like a blizzard. We watched the Casper channel until 1964 when we also received a Cheyenne channel. We often ate supper from our TV trays and ate the frozen, ready to eat TV dinners or chicken pot pies.

Northern Gas came in 1944 and Carbon County Gas and a direct dial telephone system arrived in 1953.

The Town of Saratoga was also enjoying new improvements. A sewer system was built in 1946. All cesspools were disposed of by the spring of 1950. Then the burning of trash in covered barrels was instituted. Unburnable items were hauled to the town dump which was located on a side hill north of the fairgrounds. Scavengers had a delightful time looking for usable items.

Flies and mosquitoes had plagued the town for years. Flies abated after horse droppings and outhouses were eliminated, but mosquitoes still ruined much of the summer. Tourists complained bitterly and often cut their visits short. It was impossible to enjoy any outdoor activity and people often said that we should name the mosquito as our state bird.

Mayor I.M. Conness addressed the mosquito problem in 1926 by pouring oil into the sloughs around town. Instead of millions of mosquitoes, there were thousands. Purple Martens and Gambusia Fish hardly touched the problem. Aerial spraying with Scourge took control of the mosquitoes in 1992.

The Legion leased the fairgrounds in 1931 and purchased it in 1937. People came from far and wide to their Fourth of July rodeos for many years. The Auxiliary ran a hot dog and hamburger stand and the men sold beer at the two and three-day rodeos. Dances were held at the Firemen's Hall each evening.

It was all so exciting, the author remembers. A bright cowboy shirt was purchased at Whitney's each year and decked out in western attire she sat on the fence or in the bleachers. She was especially enthralled with the horse races and Billy Jean Nixon, who won every horse race that she ran in. Cowboys came from all over the country to try their hand at saddle and bareback bronco riding, bulldogging and calf roping. Bill Whitney and Al Baum were our cowboy heroes.

Cars lined the streets every evening, each one vying for the best place to watch the promenade of gamblers, fishermen, hay hands and timber workers who were "out on a toot." There were always drunken fights, and a one-armed pimp directed customers to Kay's place in the top story of the Wolf Annex. Many attended the movies in those days. Ranchers always came in to shop for groceries, so the three or four grocery stores stayed open on Saturday nights and during the July 4th festivities.

High School Band on parade, ca. 1943

In the earlier days, food and beer stands lined the streets and the sound of ringing slot machines and firecrackers filed the air. In later years all of these activities were banned and it wasn't nearly as much fun.

Dancing has been one of our most popular events, although not as popular now as in the past. People danced in homes, country schools and Jensen Hall in the early days, with music furnished by local musicians. Jensen Hall was remodeled into a movie theater by the Legion, but the Firemen's Hall, once the Windsor Stable, became our community center when the Volunteer Fire Department bought and remodeled it. It was the site of many gatherings and dances. The hall was located on the lot south of Shively Hardware.

We danced everywhere: in the bars with music from a jukebox, at the annual Calico Ball and dinner dances given by the Lions Club and the Legion, at Sinclair Hotel's Fountain Room,

Ten Mile and Encampment City Hall. Elk Mountain's Garden Spot Pavilion's spring floor was a favorite summer destination; big bands stopped there while traveling on coast to coast tours. After the Saratoga Inn opened, that was a special dance place.

There were movies at the Range Theater nearly every night of the week; kids paid ten cents admission, and popcorn and pop were five cents each. We watched wonderful musicals, as well as Gene Autry and Roy Rogers films and knew little about the world except by newspaper, magazines and a short nightly radio broadcast. We raptly watched cartoons and a newsreel before the main feature. In the days before radio (1925) and moving pictures Margaret Pearson, who lived on Cow Creek Lane, said it was a week after the World War I Armistice that they learned the war was over.

…

The 1950's and 1960's were good years. Our industries were doing well and we were enjoying a higher standard of living, sending our children off to college and traveling as often as possible. Some people owned RV trailers.

We flocked as often as possible to the Saratoga Inn for dinner, entertainment and dancing. Dressed in our best we ate charcoal-broiled steaks, baked potatoes with sour cream and chives, and a large green salad with the new thousand island dressing. We thought we were pretty special when we were served wine—Blue Nun and Rose'—with our dinner. We were no longer country hicks.

Old Baldy Club opened in 1964, and some of the town's upper crust became members. The 18-hole golf course was one of the finest in the country. The Inn and Old Baldy gave many job opportunities.

Bridge Street in downtown Saratoga, Wyoming, in late 1950's or early 1960's. Looking East towards Kennaday Peak, center of picture in distance. Palace Hotel on left with Sisson (Wolf) Hotel on right.

North side of Bridge Street in downtown Saratoga, facing west in mid-1950's.

Outdoor recreation became more important to us. In 1950 a cut was made to bring river water to a new fish pond development northeast of town. The Lions took it on as a project and Saratoga Lake opened in 1951 with a big boat regatta. It has been a favorite year-round fishing destination for many years.

The nearby Storer Wetlands project is a bird watching paradise. The campground is administered by the town.

Saratoga Lions and Platte Valley Game and Fish Club building dock at Saratoga Lake.

1965-1990

Dramatic changes in our thinking and the way we lived began in the mid-1960's and continued into the 1980's. Color television brought the world into our living rooms and American consciousness was jolted by the assassinations of President John F. Kennedy, Martin Luther King and Bobby Kennedy. We watched escalation of the Vietnam War in Southeast Asia. Exploration in space widened our world as we watched man's first walk on the moon.

The Pill was developed in 1965 and was widely spread by the early 1970's. Old-time patriotism was on edge, produced by war protests and draft dodging that resulted in the Hippie Movement with its long hair and sloppy clothing. Peace and love were its watchwords. The draft was abolished in 1973.

The old rules of proper dress and action gradually disappeared. Suits and ties for men, plus hats, glove, matching handbags and shoes for women went out the window, along with Emily Post's big book on etiquette. New freedoms of choice emerged; divorce, illegitimacy, gay rights and unmarried couples living together became acceptable. It has been a difficult transition.

Betty Friedan's book The Feminine Mystique preached freedom and self fulfillment for women. By the 1970's half of the women worked outside of the home; wash and wear fabrics, heated homes, modern appliances and new packaged and frozen foods made this possible. Daycare and other programs were instituted and women could own their own credit card.

Saratoga, ca. 1970. Cadwell Slough at bottom of picture snakes its way to the North Platte River past the Saratoga Inn and golf course, under the S&E railroad trestle and the bridge to Veterans Island (middle left). On the Platte River two bridges appear: the improved Bridge Street Bridge and the 1949 bridge on Highway 130/230.

HANNA COAL BOOM (1973-1985)

The 1973 Arab oil embargo caused a great need for power plant fuel. Hanna's low sulphur coal was in immediate demand and mines were quickly organized. Hundreds of workers poured in. Hanna could not house all of them, so Carbon County towns became bedroom communities. It was predicted that the mines would prosper for twenty years. Our returning Vietnam veterans were pleased by the job opportunities and the high wages of 17 to 20 dollars an hour at the mines.

Saratoga was ill-prepared for this sudden influx of people. Its water and sewer system was old and could barely provide service to the new subdivisions that sprang up. Construction companies built apartments and houses for the new residents.

Inflation began and rose higher and higher. Home prices rose from $12,000.00 to $30,000.00. The Town's budget doubled to one million dollars, and it had received funding rights of ten million dollars for new water, sewer and street projects. A bond for a new high school was passed in 1978 to accommodate the doubled school enrollment. The Town's population had also doubled to over 2,200 by 1980.

A new ozone water plant, a dental and medical facility, fire department expansion, another bank, a new motel and a self-service gas and convenience store, two more churches, Valley Super on the south hill, the Senior Center and County Library were built.

Recreation for the new energetic citizens required baseball parks for the large baseball league. Snowmobiling and trail biking greatly expanded with easy credit available for machines.

Saratoga buzzed like a beehive day and night. A new all-night club named the Brass Rail opened north of town. Wyoming's drinking age had been lowered to age 19 in 1973, perhaps as a favor to returning Vietnam veterans, but that age limit returned to 21 in 1988.

Parents of teenage children looked on with horror and confusion as their children crawled out of their bedroom windows at night to join Saratoga's raucous night life. Beer keggers and house parties were common; the adult community thought that if the youth were allowed to drink beer, they wouldn't be tempted to try the new and mysterious drugs.

The Hanna coal boom peaked in 1981 then steadily went downhill until 1985 when it ended. There was still some need for coal, but Powder River coal with its thick seams near the surface was less expensive to mine.

Miners moved to greener pastures, leaving homes, trailers, snowmobiles and pickups mortgaged and unpaid for. Our two banks went under and there were confirmed and near bankruptcies. Those who stayed here dealt with continued inflation and high interest rates of 18 to 20 percent.

The new energy darlings were natural gas and oil. Drilling went into high gear south of Wamsutter in the Red Desert. Many of our unemployed miners found jobs there or at the expanding Sinclair's oil refinery.

Grant monies were in the bank for Saratoga water, sewer and street improvements when our young mayor, David Pennock, and a passenger were tragically killed in October 12, 1983. Dave's plane crashed at the William Sidley ranch on upper Cow Creek. Everyone grieved.

Vice mayor of the Town Council, Joe Glode, was left to take up the reins. He said his vigorous council members—Dorman Ewing, Randy Raymer, Dick Bradshaw and Sue Jones—worked hard to complete the huge project. It was accomplished in 1989.

There were drainage problems. Hugus ditch had to be lined with concrete. Swamps needed draining. Disheartening mud bogs, deep trenches, closed streets! The Town was full of duck ponds; the police car became stuck twice a day. What a mess!

HEALTH

Life and death issues have been grim realities faced by mankind since its beginnings. Most people lived in poverty, and famines and plagues were constant fears for many centuries.

As the 20th century began, viruses and bacteria had been identified, and sterile methods developed. Isolation of communicable diseases was proven successful.

When brides came west in the 1880's they were told to bring three books: a Bible, a cookbook and a doctor book. They also brought healing recipes that had been passed down through the generations.

Doctors were scarce, but women healer-midwives Miriam Baggott, Ann Parr, and Grandma Dillard trudged or rode miles to tend families in times of birth, death and distress. They carried kits filled with supplies and had learned their healing craft from predecessors. They were a wise and comforting presence to frightened households.

Infant mortality was high. When Iva Sowder was born prematurely, her experienced grandmother placed her in a shoebox and into the cook stove's warming oven, and the child thrived. Babies and young children often died from croup or pneumonia.

Scarlet fever, small pox, diphtheria, tetanus, whooping cough, measles, chicken pox, and polio were common. The Ryans lost their small daughters to whooping cough in the 1880's. The Horns lost their son to spinal meningitis after he went out too soon after a bout of measles. The Measons lost their 16-year-old daughter to a long unknown disease—perhaps it was diabetes.

When the Wiants lost two children to scarlet fever, the newspaper printed the following remedy: "One grain (60 mg) sulphate of zinc, one grain foxglove mixed with two tablespoons of water and four ounces of water added. Take one tablespoon every hour, with smaller doses for children." The local druggist took the zinc and foxglove from his shelves and prepared them with morter and pestle.

Vaccines were developed for these dreaded diseases by 1955, and insulin for diabetes had been discovered in 1921. Bayer Aspirin, considered a miracle drug, was available over the counter in 1912; it replaced whiskey and opium-based medicines. Sulpha was used after 1935 and penicillin after World War II. Nursing became a revered occupation after World War II. A magnetic healer visited Saratoga around 1890; she must have been a predecessor to chiropractic and massage therapy.

There was no shortage of doctors; some of them were quacks who had received only a few months of school. Mail order patent medicines contained alcohol and opium and were popular until 1915 when they were outlawed.

Our good Doctors Browder, Price and Irwin and Corbett were dedicated and used their knowledge, experience and common sense, although their methods were sometimes questionable. Doctor Price, around 1900, proclaimed "Turpentine is good internally, externally and eternally." Turpentine and lard were used for chest packs, and turpentine, sugar and water helped coughs. Before x-rays and modern technology, doctors only had fever thermometers, stethoscopes and tongue depressors, plus their experience to aid them. Treatments before the advent of sulpha were often castor oil, sarsaparilla spring tonic, enemas and iodine.

Doctors could pull teeth, visiting dentists came occasionally, and eyeglasses were selected at Scott's Jewelry in the early century.

Warren Edwards, Saratoga harness and saddle maker, developed a serious infection when he pierced his hand with an awl. He was transported by train to Denver for medical treatment and his arm was saved. Gone were the days of bloodletting and amputation. Joint replacements became available around the 1960's. Until then wheelchairs and crutches was commonplace.

The aged and destitute lived at the county's "poor farm" at Savery in the Snake River Valley in the early days. Kendall's Home for the Aged served Saratoga for many years. The 50-bed Valley View Manor was built by the Larry Vyveys and Kendall McBrides in 1974.

Carbon County Memorial Hospital was built in Rawlins in 1921. Valley residents purchased an ambulance in 1963. Don Herold drove it and became the first trained EMT. Dr. and Mrs. John Johnson built a dental and medical clinic in 1980; our beloved Dr. John Lunt (1977-1998) practiced there until the Corbett Medical Clinic was built in 1996.

R. A. Corbett, M. D., Saratoga's doctor 1934-1972

The clinic was named for Dr. Ray A. Corbett who came here in 1934 and practiced until 1972. He personified the American folk hero, the country doctor, who was always on call to make house and ranch calls any day and any hour, and he could deal with any emergency — there we few specialists in these parts.

Dr. Corbett graduated from the University of Wyoming in 1929, got his medical degree from the University of Michigan, and took two years of surgical training in Dayton, Ohio. He said that he especially enjoyed delivering babies and surgery. When there was a doctor shortage during World War II he performed 90 percent of the surgeries at the Rawlins hospital.

Once upon a time the elderly lived with their children but now Social Security (1936), Medicare (1965), Medicaid, Unemployment Compensation (1939) and health insurance take care of the elderly and the sick. Modern health care is very costly, but people live longer thanks to diagnostic procedures, improved diets, and healthier living.

The valley presently has difficulty hiring a doctor, providing emergency care and has a failing nursing home. The town has plans to build a large facility that will solve these problems.

EDUCATION

How can we progress without an education? America, the land of equal opportunity, has always valued education. Not every country has free public schooling.

Isadore Bolton, who developed much of the Bolton-Werner-Overland Trail ranch, was an early 1900's immigrant from Russia. He was not given education there because he was a Jew. He knew he needed to figure, read and write if he was going to make progress here; he prowled schools and libraries seeking help, and he learned. He married a librarian.

There was an amazing mixture of accents and people from other countries in the valley—people from Sweden, Norway, Finland, Denmark, Germany, Russia, Bohemia, Belgium, Poland,

Czechoslovakia and Britain. They shared their rich cultures and taught their children to value their educations.

In 1880 William Cadwell, married with a son, led the way to education when he helped lay out eleven school districts in the valley. Nine were country schools. A charming white school house was built in Saratoga in 1889.

Saratoga's first school opened in 1889 with 18 students. The school hosted the Kling country school children on October 12, 1892 to celebrate 400 years since Columbus landed in America. Pictured with their teacher Lida Hood are: B.T. Ryan, W.E. Meason, W.H. Kling, J.C. Brewer and Maxwell children who gave patriotic recitations for the event. The Kling School served students on the river from the mouth of Cedar Creek to Elk Hollow Ranch. The Saratoga school was located east of the river on a lot north of the present Silver Moon Motel.

Country school fathers built one-room log schools in the designated school districts, each one administered by an elected school board. The schools were also used for elections, meeting and social gatherings. They were gradually abandoned as roads and transportation improved.

Country school teachers were scarce with some young and ill-prepared. The first schools were poorly funded. Teachers boarded with ranch families. A county Superintendent of Schools held a week of training in Rawlins each fall and visited the country schools where they supervised teachers and curriculum.

Opening day for 1900 school. A brick 2-story school was built on the west hill in 1900. There were four large classrooms and two wide halls in the center. Four pot-bellied stoves heated the classrooms. Somewhere out of sight there is an outhouse. (The Canis-Wiant and the Hugus-Stolns are on the left background.)

Parents encouraged and added to their children's education in many ways. Margaret Sullivan Pearson said that families on lower Cow Creek each bought two or three books each year that were traded back and forth. The author recalls the bookcase filled with Zane Gray and other novels from the 1920's and 1930's that had been given to her family, and the Book(s) of Knowledge purchased around 1940. Newspapers and many magazines, the Montgomery Ward and Sears Roebuck catalogs were all well-used. Cards and letters often passed through the mail. (After telephones arrived, they were used only for serious long distance calls since long distance calls were expensive.)

The first schools were not compulsory and were open to students 6 to 21 years of age. They were poorly funded until more tax monies became available from developed ranches, homes, businesses and livestock. The first schools had two-month terms. Six month terms began in 1903, and nine month terms began in 1923, when oil and gas royalties were received.

Saratoga High School 1926, author's collection

Saratoga held its first four year commencement for Paul Breniman in 1924. He was an upper Cedar Creek ranch boy who had attended country school, but he worked for John Paulson in the Paulson Medicinal Well bottling works and boarded at the Paulson home during his high school years. School principal Duerig recognized Paul's potential and knew his desire for higher education and guided Paul through the needed graduation requirements. An elated and proud crowd attended Paul's ceremony at Jensen Hall. Mrs. Seal, who played piano for the silent movies, played for Paul that night, he remembered.

Our first high school opened in 1926. A large brick elementary school was erected by Spiegelburg in 1928. A smaller than regulation gym and a stage were in the center, with classrooms on the east and west. Balconies hung from the walls. Basketball, PE, plays and graduation exercises were held there.

1928 Elementary School, author's collection. Purple and gold became the school colors at the suggestion of Ken Day, Class of '27. He explained that those colors would be good because they were regal colors.

A regulation gym, now a part of the Platte Valley Community Center, was built in 1954. More school sports—wrestling and volleyball—were introduced then. The school lunch room began as a WPA project during the depression — a hot soup lunch for ten cents was served.

Memories of those happy school days flood in: watching the older boys play marbles for "keepsies or funsies" while the other children played Run Sheep Run, hop-scotch or jump rope, candy showers for the teacher, weeklong freshmen initiation with one-way rides, funny costumes and skits, Halloween and April

Fool's Day pranks, slumber parties, school dances, and crowding into Donelan Drug Store booths for cherry cokes, milk shakes and ice cream sodas.

There were naughty tricks also. Marian Aden smeared skunk oil on the high school's radiator heaters, and school was dismissed for the day. A favorite Halloween trick was tipping over outhouses (once with someone in it), plus burning one on the bridge. A wagon was hoisted onto the Western Wear roof. Joe Gaspari drove his motorcycle into the high school on a pre-graduation day. Kelly Evans was hostess to a cocktail party that preceded the Junior Senior banquet and prom in 1980. Jungle juice in a big iron kettle on the lawn was served in wine glasses to the well-dressed guests. "It was classy," a junior girl said. The best trick occurred in 1975, when Loy Russell was bribed with a case of beer and $50.00 to streak through the gym; he ran so fast that hardly anyone saw him, except Sun photographer Carrie Craig who quickly snapped him, and his picture was published the next week—with a fig leaf. Teachers and parents seemed to enjoy our imaginative antics.

Part of the elementary school was built in 1951, the present high school in 1980, and the adjoining gym in 1990.

Carbon County consolidated its schools into two districts in 1971-72 with Saratoga in the east half and the District Two office established here. Country schools were eliminated; the Brush Creek and Ryan Park schools were our last.

Today's students seem to find learning a fun and interesting experience. They are busy with improved curriculums, more athletics and exciting modern technology.

A computer was installed in the district office in 1972 and a satellite in 1974. An experimental five year technology plan began in 1977 that transformed education and prepared students for a changing world.

Tiresome subjects like penmanship, Latin and shorthand are long gone. There are now enrichment classes—music, art, drama, industrial arts. Students can go on line and receive college credits. Counseling is available, and research is computerized. Girls have been very involved in sports since 1972. Once upon a time girls had few career opportunities. Most felt that nursing, teaching, and secretarial work were their only options, but girls take any of a multitude of majors now.

Elementary students receive special help through remedial reading (1966), speech therapy and special education. Early education is important; kindergarten started up around 1962, and Preschool and Headstart have since been added.

CHAPTER SEVEN

Later Changes

1980-2000

The valley and nation went through the difficult 1980's with its usual spirit and optimism. Saratoga looked and felt much better after the street, water and sewer projects were finished.

We were cheered by a new Senior Center, Carbon County Library and Saratoga High School. A two per cent lodging tax was passed.

The Saratoga/Platte Valley Chamber of Commerce had been formed in 1974. In 1984 Chuck Box, now a well-known author, had graduated from the University of Denver with a degree in journalism and was working as a reporter for the Saratoga Sun when he was asked to head the Chamber. He accepted but soon discovered there was not enough money in the treasury to pay his salary.

As Box and Ralph Bartholomew, local pharmacist and Chamber president, were walking down the street one day, they hit upon a money-making project—a January Ice Fishing Derby at Saratoga Lake. They had hoped for 400 participants but had 1,600, all vying for two tagged fish named Steve and Bob, each worth $25,000.00. This popular three-day event is held each year;

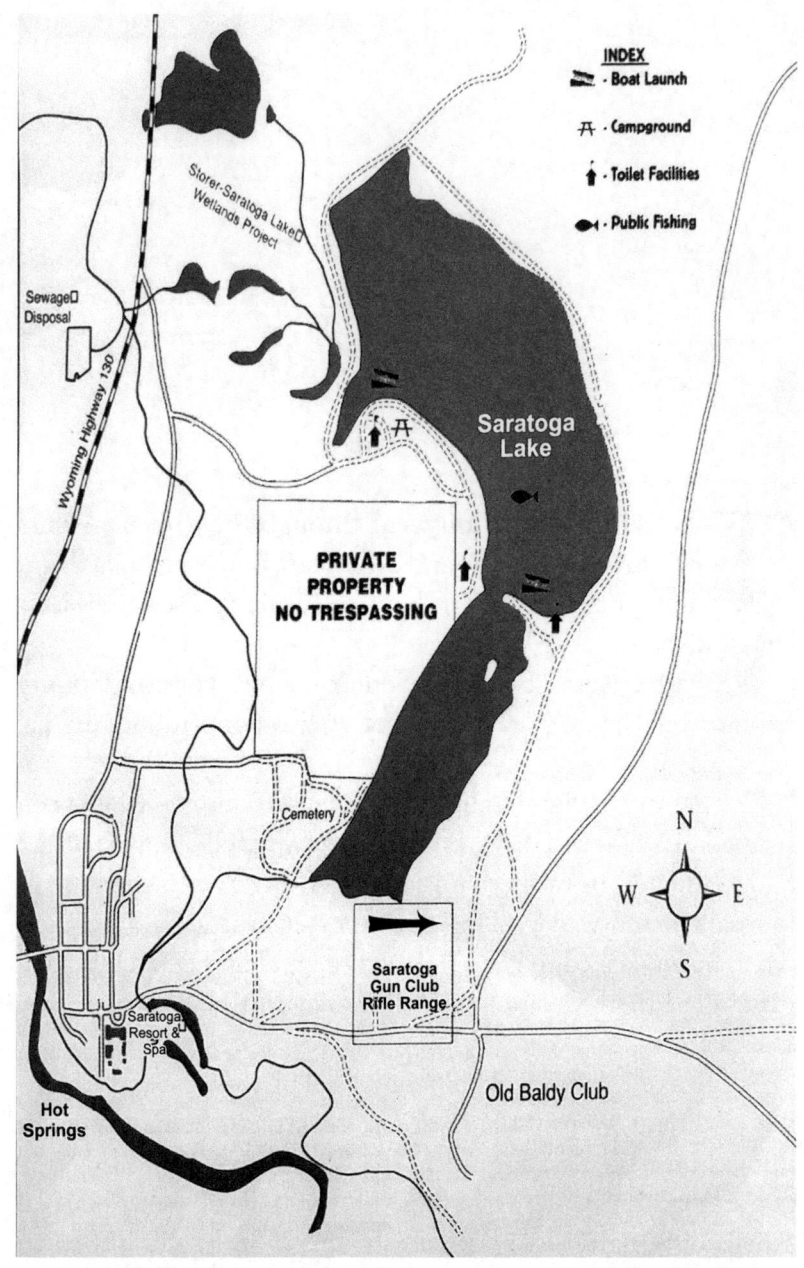

Saratoga Lake Recreation Area, courtesy of The Saratoga Sun

changes in rules and prizes have made it even more enjoyable

Since that time more and more winter and summer events have been added to entertain valley residents and visitors. It was aptly named "The Good Times Valley" by Chamber president Nancy Pennock, and Rick Hughes described it nicely when he said, "Where else can you fish, hunt, golf and soak all in the same day?" The valley was becoming a great year round tourist destination.

In the 1990's businesses and homes were spruced up with bright paint. Old fashioned street lights and brick patterned sidewalks greatly enhanced the downtown. Outflow from the Hot Pool heated icy sidewalks on the north side of the street. The Town bought the parking lot south of the Hotel Wolf and paved and landscaped it. A large gazebo graced the museum grounds.

The Valley Chapel was built at the cemetary in 1999 and expanded and enclosed in 2002. Many memorial services are held there. A peaceful and comforting view of the mountains can be seen through the big east windows.

Saratoga Cemetary Valley Chapel, photo courtesy of Cindy Loose

Saratoga had greatly expanded from the river bottom flood lands to the west and south bench lands during and after the 1970's. A large trailer park, storage facilities and construction companies were built on the west hill, and new businesses sprouted along the highway to the south. Two gas and convenience stores replaced filling stations. Realty companies, flower shops, an improved Hotel Wolf, art galleries, clothing and gift shops and other supportive businesses appeared. Rawlins National Bank built a beautiful new building on First Street in 1996.

Our medical clinic was outgrowing its space in the Johnson dental building in 1994. Gretchen Swanson Velde gave $50,000.00 toward a medical foundation that would support a new clinic. Her son Kurt Bucholz headed the board. More large donations came in and the new Corbett Medical Center opened in 1996. (Velde had visited the valley since the 1940's and had purchased the XH Ranch from Paul and Alice Holms in 1957.)

The Corbett Medical Center ribbon cutting, ca. 1996. Pictured are Dr. John Lunt, Dr. Kurt Bucholz, Bessie and John Bucholz.

Saratoga began receiving national praise in 1995 when a widely read magazine named Men's Journal featured Saratoga as one of eight "Pieces of Paradise" in the Rocky Mountain region—its Hobo Pool and river floating excursions were mentioned.

Other magazines were equal in praise in following years.

Travel magazine talked about the slower pace, the friendly people, the night life and strolling down the main street. An internet database named Saratoga as one of the best places to buy a second home. The vacated houses from the coal bust were purchased for weekend and summer retreats.

2000-2020

The first two decades of the 21st century began with drought, a 100 year flood and forest fires—a time when we became well acquainted with a new term—Global Warming.

A blowdown of 6 million trees north of Steamboat, Colorado occurred in October, 1997, and we were warned against a huge infestation of Mountain Pine Beetles coming our way.

Trees had been stressed by a decade of drought, warm winters and fire suppression for nearly 100 years. Forests were overgrown and thick and 88% of our lodgepole pines were 50 to 75 years old. The beetles would multiply quickly under those conditions.

By 2000 we could see red and brown trees that turned into grey skeletons, and forest fires became a threat throughout the Rocky Mountain region. We anxiously watched the horizon for signs of smoke and sprayed the needle trees in our yards to save them. The drought and beetle epidemic ended by 2012. We have been spared from fires in our immediate area with the nearest one south of Big Creek Ranch.

We had a 100-year flood in 2011 that threatened river bank homes and businesses. Specialists were brought in. A fluvial geomorphologist said that the river widens between the two bridges and that a narrower, deeper channel would create the water velocity that was needed to move the bed load through town. But the project would take a study and the final cost could be in the millions of dollars.

Water problems of another nature appeared around 2002.

There had been a shortage of residential water since the 1950's—people were often restricted from watering their lawns. River water had been used for some time but quantity and quality were in question. Ground water from the North Park Aquifer, northeast of Saratoga near the Pennock Mountain Wildlife Refuge, was tested and approved. Three wells were drilled and the water was delivered to the growing Saratoga in 2008-2009.

*Flooding banks of the North Platte River,
photo courtesy of Cindy Loose*

   Is there another town that has a dirt and river rock quarry within its town limits? Many truckloads for landscaping have been hauled away since 2005.
   The Town, like others in Wyoming, suffered from economic instability in 2000 and the state needed solutions. The Town, Chamber of Commerce and Carbon County requested an assessment from the Wyoming Rural Development. It resolved that this was a valley with fine attributes and that a community center that fostered social, education, recreation and business to diversify our economy was needed.
   A seven-member joint powers board (CCJPB) was formed with Joe Glode as chairman and Stacy Crimmins vice chairman.

Initially, they found a possible site on the bench above the Hot Pool and began making plans. However, such plans changed.

In 2005 the state targeted our schools that had been expanded during the mining boom. The state wanted to cut footage down to 30 square foot per student. The state would pay for demolition of the beloved 1928 grade school and addition. There would be an addition to the elementary school and seventh and eighth graders would be moved to the oversized high school. The school donated the land in exchange for use of the community center facilities which would be located on Elm Street.

The center was an expensive and formidable challenge if needs and wants were to be achieved. The new building, 27,500 square feet in size, and remodeling of the gymnasium facility would cost around six million dollars.

Two large donors came forward at this time: Peter Storer and Kurt Bucholz each gave one million dollars from family foundations. Bucholz was a state representative and on the Wyoming Business Council; he is credited for bringing two state grants totaling two and a half million dollars to the project.

Construction began in June 2006 and massive fundraising began. Donations poured in from pockets of any size—room naming for five thousand to five hundred thousand to theater seats for five hundred dollars and bricks for fifty dollars. Inflation raised the building price another half million dollars. Undaunted, the Platte Valley Community Center

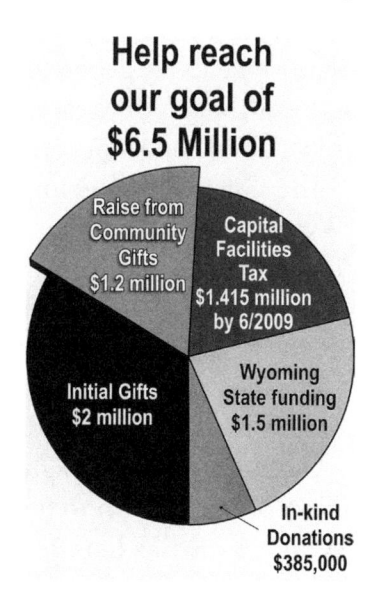

Help reach our goal of $6.5 Million

- Raise from Community Gifts $1.2 million
- Capital Facilities Tax $1.415 million by 6/2009
- Wyoming State funding $1.5 million
- In-kind Donations $385,000
- Initial Gifts $2 million

board moved on.

The building was designed by Rick Morton from Colorado. Delta Construction from Laramie was the building contractor. But after the building was finished, there were more needs—landscaping, parking lot and furnishings. The Town took charge of landscaping.

Platte Valley Community Center, photo courtesy Joe Elder, PVCC

The Platte Valley Community Center was completed September 21, 2007. It was a remarkable seven year, eight million dollar project.

There is a PVCC foundation and funds for maintenance and improvements are generated each year by silent and live auctions at the birthday bashes each September. Summer residents as well as locals have shown great generosity.

The Chamber of Commerce office staff acts as hostess. A PVCC manager and maintenance man keep the place running efficiently.

It is the community's pride and joy and it more than satisfies the social, education, recreational and business goals.

During this period tourism increased and there were other significant changes.

Carbon Power and Light built a new facility in 2007 and the Town government moved into their vacated building on Spring Avenue. Dr. Mike Janssen purchased the Saratoga Inn in 2008, renamed it Saratoga Resort and Spa, and made some remarkable improvements.

Technology has exploded in this 21st century. The World Wide Web brings information on any subject. People carry IPhones or Smartphones everywhere they go. People regularly take school classes, shop, conduct business and work over the internet. They advertise and sell, shop for homes, automobiles, groceries and a huge variety of items.

The North Platte Valley Medical Center when completed will be a dream come true. It will serve as the valley's nursing home, 24-hour emergency with overnight care, clinical care, visiting doctors and rehab services. The U.S. Department of Agriculture will help fund the project, and operational expenses will be subsidized by Medicare. It will be administered as a 501(c)(3) non-profit. Paul McCarthy has given land on the west hill, a doctor has been hired, and fundraising has begun. Will Faust leads the project.

2020 brings important challenges: a coronavirus pandemic, racial and monetary problems, continuous wars, nasty political division and global warming. Perhaps the words from Maude Willford, our early historian who was born in 1882, can ground and guide us in the difficult years ahead: "Our pioneers were resourceful, high-spirited, optimistic, resilient and independent. Their goal was not riches, but a good home—permanent and something to be proud of. No glory, fame or notoriety."

IT TAKES A VILLAGE

Saratoga is a friendly place. Wherever we gather—at the post office, the grocery story or the Hot Pool—we get smiles and hellos that lift the spirit and brighten the day. No one is left out—we love our town full of interesting characters, each one with a story to tell.

Neighbors helping neighbors and strangers helping strangers.

We need each other. This is a place where you are not judged by the clothes you wear or the money in your pocket.

An army of volunteers keeps this village running. We could not function without them. Mayors and council receive little compensation for their large responsibilities, and all of those who serve on boards are volunteers. Our business owners give generously to any cause, activity or event.

Many fundraising and entertaining events are held each year in the valley—all with volunteer effort. A valuable feeling of camaraderie and self-giving are their rewards. We have had wonderful organizations that have led these events—recently the Lions Club, the Chamber of Commerce, the Valley Service Organization, the Platte Valley Arts Council, Helping Hands, Saratoga Museum and the American Legion and Auxiliary. We are extremely proud of our nine churches, food pantry, and thrift store.

Saratoga Lions Club members, Hank Jewel, Doug Campbell and Rocky Fiedor serve at community center picnic fundraiser, photo courtesy of Cindy Loose

The Saratoga Lions Club has been the most loyal and hardworking organization since it was chartered in 1928. The club members meet for a dinner meeting every Thursday evening and are guided by an experienced board of directors who meet separately and recommend projects—this avoids long meetings and needless conflict. The club has given generously to various causes but is best-known for its work on Saratoga Lake, Veterans Island and Buck Springs. They have cooked and fed 1,000 people many times and are always willing to work on other projects.

Saratoga has always had strong leadership. Wilbur B. Hugus and Fenimore C. Chatterton were probably our first. They could inspire folks to give their best because they were trusted.

F. O. Williams

Frank Williams, a Calf Creek rancher, was in the first State Senate (1890) when there were only five counties. Many important men ate at the (Henry) Jones and Williams ranch table. Among them was Elwood Mead who is credited for Wyoming's water laws. The State Constitution was written and important legislation was passed during those early years.

L.G. Davis was also an early legislator. He was the first

supervisor of the Medicine Bow National Forest (1902), a U.S. Wyoming Marshal and a founding director, then a president of Saratoga State Bank (1899). His ranch was the present Kelley Land and Cattle Company on the river; Davis brought in 100 head of the first Registered Herefords.

Captain L. G. Davis, legislator, US Marshall and Rough Rider with President Theodore Roosevelt, ca. 1916

Leaders spend long days and sleepless nights while formulating plans. Their word is always good. There were many selfless leaders throughout the years. Some that come to mind are Fred Healey, Elton Trowbridge and Kendall McBride; but there were others.

Few people remember S.S. Sharp. He grew up in Sheridan and while studying Latin and Greek at the University of Wyoming received the revered Rhodes scholarship to Oxford University in England. While pointing artillery guns during World War I

S. S. Sharp

he studied mathematics and field manuals, and on the strength of what he had learned passed the Civil Engineering test and was hired by the State Water Engineer's office. He surveyed the waters of the North Platte River in the upper North Platte River Valley and was chief witness in the important Colorado-Wyoming-Nebraska water lawsuit. He loved the valley's air and open space and came here to live in 1924. He was musical, started a dance band and while teaching high school advanced mathematics during the World War II teacher shortage, he started Saratoga's first school band. He was a master surveyor, respected by all. Sharp was Saratoga's mayor for about 14 years; during his term he laid out the airport and unlocked the mysteries of Saratoga Hot Springs. Money was never his goal, only achievement.

The modest Don Herold served as fire chief of the Saratoga Volunteer Fire Department for 49 years. He drove our first ambulance and was our first trained EMT. Many people in crisis have been helped by his efforts.

Don Herold

Joe Glode is a natural leader and problem solver. He has the ability to inspire talented people into action. He led the way during the huge 1980's water, sewer and street improvement projects and brought the Platte Valley Community Center to completion. If you have a problem go talk with Joe.

Watch out for Dick Perue. His constant enthusiasm is contagious. When you go to Dick's house he always has a table full of projects he is working on—a historical trek, program or event with pictorial history handouts. Many people come to his doorstep for pictures and help and are always welcomed. His promise to his mentor Bob Martin will be honored totally when the thousands of pictures from the Martin collection and his own large collection are digitalized and sent into "the cloud" for everyone's use.

Joe Glode

Dick Perue

Laura M

"Laura M" Marrow received the Wyoming Women of Influence Business of the Year award in 2018. She has worked tirelessly in her very successful clothing, art and gifts business and for Saratoga since she came here in 1996. Crazy Days, Festival of the Arts, Farmers Market, fashion shows and open houses with lots of food have been held under her energetic direction.

Loren "Teense" Willford has entertained us for years with his guitar, voice and humor, and he has emceed at parades, memorials and football games. His Wyoming Homegrown band plays for valley resorts and events throughout the nation.

Teense Willford

We have had much more than our share of musical entertainers, artists and authors. They have enlightened our lives.

Virginia F. Large captured valley scenes with her oils in the 1940's and 1950's. Skip Glomb, Robert Finney, Jerry Palen and Dawn Senior Trask have since been popular artists. There are also some very fine craftsmen.

Noted local artist Virginia Frederick Large, ca. 1966.

Our authors, too, have been many: Fenimore C. Chatterton and W.L. Kuykendal were our earliest, followed by Maude Wenonah Willford, Gay Day Alcorn, Candy Vyvey Moulton, Lori Van Pelt, Chuck Larsen and Chuck Box.

It takes a lot of great people to make a village a home. We're proud to say we are from Saratoga, Wyoming!

Index

A Bar A Ranch 100
Aden, Marian 140
Agassiz, L. 32
Airplanes 95
Airport 97
Alcorn, Gay Acknowledgments
American Legion 55, 107, 115, 124, 152
Angus England 107
Anschutz Corp. 70
Antelope 80
Automobiles 91, 122

Baker, Jim 3, 4
Banks 55, 154
Barkhurst, Jessie 55
Bartlett, Chuck Acknowledgments
Baum, Al 124
Bartholomew, Ralph 143
Bensen, Len Acknowledgments, 85
Bolton, I. 67-70, 136
Bonfil, Fred 84
Bordellos (Willis) 34
Box, Chuck 143, 160
Bradshaw, Dick 132
Brauer, Bill 21
Breniman, Paul Acknowledgments 109, 139
Brewer, John, 29, 60, 137
Burdick-Chatterton 55 93
Brush Creek Ranch 100
Brush Creek Ranger Station 77, 113
Bucholz, Kurt 146, 149
Buck Springs 153

Cadwell, William 21-28, 104, 136
Campbell, Doug 152
Carbon 20
Carbon County Acknowledgments
Carbon County Fair 51

Carbon Power and Light 150, 121
Carbon County Hospital 134
Cattle 60-67
Cattle Mutilation 70
Cemeteries 32, 50
Chamber of Commerce 143, 150, 152
Chatterton, Fenimore 24-30, 35, 40, 62, 153
Christman, Kelly Acknowledgments
Chokecherry and Sierra Madre Wind 75
Civilian Conservation Corps 103, 113, 117, 118
Community Church 115
Conness, I. M. 124
Copeland, Jim Acknowledgments
Corbett Medical Clinic 135
Corbett, Ray 135
Corpening, Tex 11, 110, 112
Cosgriff Bros. 55
Craig, Carrie 141

Dairy 66
Dance bands 111
Dances 125
Davis, A. D. 100
Davis, L. G. 153
Depression Acknowledgments, 65, 112
Dodge, Fred 55
Doctors 133-134
    Price, Sam; Corbett, Ray 135;
    Lunt, John 146
Doggett, A. J. 55
Donelan, L. D. 98, 140

Eager, John 65
Education 1331
Edwards, W. E. 56, 134

Electricity 56, 122
Encampment Acknowledgments, 36-43
Energy (wind) 70, (coal) 70
Episcopal Church 30, 31, 34
Evans, Kelly 141
Evans, Valle Acknowledgments, 68
Ewing, D. 132

Ferguson, V. C. 31
Filling station 92
Fiedor, Rocky 152
Fireman's Hall 124-125
Firewater 32
Fish Fries 41, 83, 104
Fish Hatchery 88
Fishing 82, (float) 84-88, 146
Floods 147
Flying Diamond Ranch 109
Forest Service Acknowledgments
Fourth of July 125
Freighting 36-40, 47

Garages 92
Gaspari, Joe 140
Geology Acknowledgments, 82, 95
Germany 96
Glode, Joe Acknowledgments, 132, 157
Glomb, Skip Frontpiece
Golden Eagle 68
Gold Hill 30-36
Grubb, Renee Acknowledgments

Hanna 131
Healey, Fred 154
Healey, Grace Acknowledgments
Henderson, Don 110
Hepner, Rich Acknowledgments
Herold, Don 133, 156
Highways 94, 122
Hines Lumber 78
Hippies 128

Hobo Hot Pool 101-102, 146
Holms, Paul 146
Homesteading 58
Hood, Thomas 34, 137
Horn, Tom 24, 61
Hot Springs Acknowledgments, 2-6, 25, 103-104
Hot Springs Hotel 83
Hotel Wolf 35-36, 65, 127
Hughes, Rick 143
Hugus-Chatterton Store 22-25
Hugus Ditch 132
Hugus, J. W. 24, 55
Hugus, W. B. 22-40, 55, 153
Hunting 79
Huston, Al 60

Ice Fishing Derby 143
Improvements (Saratoga) 132
Indians 1-3, 12-19
Indian Bathtubs 2
Interstate 80 96

Janssen, Dr. Mike 150
Jensen, Gus 55
Jensen Hall 55, 125
Jewel, Hank 152
Johnson, John 135
Jones, Henry 60
Jones, Sue 132
Jones, Vivian Acknowledgments
Jones-Williams 11, 60

Kennaday Peak 99
Kinnamon, D. C. Acknowledgments
Korean War 120
Kralick, Colleen Acknowledgments
Kreigh, E. 34

Lake Marie 93
Large, V. F. 160
Latter Day Saints 11-12
Library 131

Lions Club 97, 105, 128-129, 152-153
Livestock (grazing) 77
Longhorns Acknowledgments
Loose, Cindy Acknowledgments

Malden, John 88-90
Manifest Destiny 7-9
Martin, R. D. and Mary 111
McBride, Kendall 134, 154
McCarthy, Paul 151
Meason, W. E. 57, 133, 137
Meeker Massacre 58
Medical facilities 131
Medicine Acknowledgments
Medicine Bow Lodge 76, 109
Medicine Bow National Forest 77, 79
Medicine Bow Peak 95
Memorial Day 119
Midway Acknowledgments, 37
Mining Acknowledgments
Morrow, Laura 56, 158
Mosquitoes 124
Motels 92
Mountain Pine Beetles 147
Movies 126
Mullison, John Acknowledgments, 3, 29, 79

Nixon, Billy Jean 124
Northern Gas 123
North Platte Medical Center 151
North Platte River 47, 63-66, 72, 82-88, 104, 154

Old Baldy Club Acknowledgments, 99, 126, 144
Olson, Ken 70
Oregon Trail 9-13
Overland Trail Cover, Acknowledgments, 13-20
Overland Trail Ranch 67
Paddock, David Acknowledgments

Palace Hotel 127
Patterson, Hack Acknowledgments
Paulson, John 139
Pearson, M. 138
Peck, Josh Acknowledgments
Pennock, David 132
Pennock, Nancy 143
Perue, Dick Acknowledgments, 111, 157, Back Cover
Peryam, Joe 55
Pine Beetle Epidemic 78
Plaga, Otto 109-110
Platte Valley Community Center 140, 148-150,
Platte Valley Lyre 46
Pranks 115
Presbyterian Church 34, 115-116
Price, Garrett 54, 65, 84
Prohibition 108
Prostitution 34, 45-46, 75, 116, 125

Quartzite 95

Ranching Acknowledgments
Raymer, Randy 132
Reed, W. H. 5
River Street Garage 92
Roads 91
R. R. Crow 42, 75-78
Rural Electrification REA 121
Russell, Loy 141
Ryan, B. T. "Tom" 57, 60, 75, 137
Ryan Park 76

Salt Lake City 12
Saratoga (name) 29, 146; (additions) 29; (water) 148
Saratoga and Encampment Railroad 40-43; Depot 43
Saratoga Hot Springs 100
Saratoga Inn/Resort 99-100, 126, 150
Saratoga Lake 127, 144
Saratoga Museum 43-44

Saratoga Sun Acknowledgments, 47, 110
Schools 140
Schroeder, Bill 120
Scott, C. W. 32, 46, 82
Sewer 124
Sharp, S. S. 55, 97, 101, 109, 154
Sheep 62, 64-65
Sheep Rock 65, 85
Shively Field 97, 100
Shively Hardware 30, 35-36
Shively, Jack 97
Sierra Madre Clubhouse 30, 34, 83
Silver Spur 100
Sinclair 92, 132
Sisson, Baldy 82-84
Sisson Hotel 127
Snowy Range 94-95
Soviet Union 120
Sowder, Thad 54
Spanish Flu 106
Spotted Dog 44-45
Stagecoach 39
State Bath House 100
Steamboat Acknowledgments, 51-55, 109
Stockgrowers Bank 93
Storer, George B. 99
Storer, Peter 149
Swift's Pool Hall 93, 116

TA Ranch 100
Teller, J. C. 71
Telephone 76, 124
Television 123
Ten Mile 76
Theaters 115
Tie drives 72
Tie hacks 72
Trowbridge, Elton 154
Turnbull, Butch 67, 114

Uihlien, Edgar 90

Union Pacific 20, 40, 60, 71

Valley Chapel 50, 144
Valley Super 131
Valley View Manor 134
Velde, Gretchen 146
Veteran's Island 101, 104
Vietnam 120, 131
Volunteer Fire Departement 125
Vyvey, Larry 134

Walcott 40
Walker, Bill and Pic 99
Ward, Georgia 109-110
Warm Springs 21-28
Water Acknowledgments, 63, 131
Waterloo 109
Weather 62
Werner, Herman Acknowledgments, 68
Whitneys 124
Willford, Maude 122, 151
Willford, Teense 159
Williams, Frank 153
Wilson, Roy 110
Winter of '49 66
Wolf Annex 55, 125
Wolves 67
Women 117, 129
World War I 105
World War II 116